See You Jimmy!

The humour, the people and the patter o' the Clyde shipyards

Allan Morrison

ILLUSTRATED BY

www.vitalspark.co.uk

The Vital Spark
is an imprint of
Neil Wilson Publishing Ltd
303 The Pentagon Centre
36 Washington Street
GLASGOW
G3 8AZ

Tel: 0141-221-1117
Fax: 0141-221-5363
E-mail: info@nwp.co.uk
www.nwp.co.uk

ACKNOWLEDGEMENTS
Many thanks to Bob Black, Alex and May Brown,
Raymond Brown, Jim Crumlish, Jim Findlay,
Neil Forsyth, Jimmy MacKellar, Andrew Pearson,
Michael Smith, Sir Simpson Stevenson, Eric Sutherland
and Archie Wilson.

A catalogue record for this book is available
from the British Library.

ISBN 1-903238-04-8

Typeset in Bodoni
Designed by Mark Blackadder
Printed in Finland by WS Bookwell

Contents

Introduction

The Clyde is one of Scotland's greatest natural assets: a pleasant waterway of breathtaking natural beauty, yet still surrounded in many places by the reminders of its shipbuilding heritage.

Shipyards were vast, amazing workplaces, where creations grew to eventually tower over the landscape. No one has or ever will use the expression, 'as pretty as a shipyard'. The noise, shouting, dirt and smells were overpowering. Yet despite the danger and poor working conditions, it was with great pride that some of the finest vessels in the world were produced there.

This book draws on material supplied by those who worked in the shipyards, including my own late father and grandfathers. Every yard has a memory, every worker a story. Weird and wonderful were the irreverent, humorous incidents, the patter was caustic – the humour sustained morale in times of hardship or adversity. Even today, ex-shipyard workers are able to recall, eyes sparkling as they roll back the years, the laughs they all had. It begs the question as to how did they ever manage to build ships with all the malarkey and shenanigans they got up to?

It was traditional in Clyde shipyards for workers to be given nicknames. Although general terms were used like 'Big Man', 'Wee Fellow' or 'Listen China', other names had much more interesting derivations. 'The Chinaman' was so named as he had 'wan lung': 'The Other Chinaman' had 'wan lung too'. 'Vic' tended to, well … get up your nose. 'John the Bomb' was a

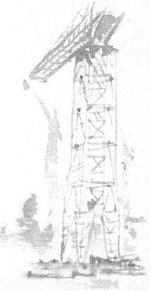

JOHN THE BOMB

gaffer who was forever exploding, as was 'MacFadyen the Bad Yin' ,who would kick over your can of tea if you started to brew up before the hooter blew. 'Naechance' tended to be a somewhat negative fellow. 'Cough-drop' was forever passing out cough drops, and 'Tuppenny's' catch-phrase was that he 'couldnae give tuppence' about anything. An apprentice, wee Jimmy Muir, who features in this book, became known as, 'See you, Jimmy', and the story behind this is:

One day, after a launch, the new ship was floating happily on the Clyde between two nudging tugs. A yard chargehand, Willie Marshall, had thrown his bunnet in the air with excitement as the ship slipped into the river and in trying to catch it again he had overbalanced and fallen into the deep, murky waters by the quayside. One of the apprentices, a well-liked young character in the yard, Jimmy Muir, unhesitatingly dived in and eventually located Willie. He dragged the half-drowned chargehand onto a slipway where, with Willie lying half-in and half-out of the water, artificial respiration was applied by young Jimmy, heaving and pushing on Willie's back.

Soon Willie spewed up a spurt of water followed by another and then another and then another ... a seemingly never-ending flow. Suddenly a booming voice was heard. It was Jimmy's foreman. 'See you, Jimmy! Get Wullie's erse oot that watter or ye'll empty the whole bliddy Clyde!' After such a public outburst it was only natural for Jimmy Muir to become, 'See you, Jimmy'. Anyway, as he soon realised, if he had just been plain Jimmy, when someone shouted 'Jimmy!' across the yard, everybody would have turned around.

BIG MAN   WEE FELLOW

1

'See the Clyde? It flows through your veins and intae yer dreams!'

Scottish humour travels well. Have we Scots not dispersed across this world to share with those less fortunate our unique mirth, cheeky expressions, high-jinks and laughter? Indeed the brash, bolshie patter from Scotland helps the world to laugh.

Much of Scottish humour originated in industry, especially the shipyards surrounding the Clyde. With so many demanding jobs where the work was dirty, dangerous and difficult, and carried out in inclement weather, it is understandable that wry and pungent humour, quick repartee and shenanigans were needed to make life tolerable. Patter and nonsense associated with bullying gaffers, petty thieving, chancers, malingerers and football, together with religious bigotry and sexual innuendo, were common themes. It was a comic sideshow of yard life, spawned by the culture of the West of Scotland. In the Clyde shipyards, vibrant and pioneering marine engineering skills competed with 'cairry oans' and daft tomfoolery, taking a rise out of apprentices and wild exploits.

The shipyards were cornucopias of colourful characters. Men and women with interests in such diverse subjects as linear algebra, Greek mythology, ancient languages, the arts and so on, who, had they had the opportunity, might have gone on to university or to achieve greatness in the world outside. Some, of course, fulfilled that potential.

By the beginning of the 20th century, a steady supply of cheap labour had helped shipbuilding play a major role in Britain's economic wealth, making Clydeside one of the foremost manufacturing regions of the world. Engineering, building and dredging works shaped the flow of the modern river. More than 30 shipyards employed thousands of people on the Clyde. The shipyards grew rapidly, soaring to a record output of 756,800 tons in 1913. With an estimated 36,000 or more ships built on the Clyde since shipbuilding began, the river was at one time the most prolific in the world. However, the end of World War One marked the start of a decline as naval disarmament and cheap competition from abroad overshadowed the following years. World War Two sustained the industry in the short term, but from 1945 onwards it could no longer match the foreign competition and suffered from a lack of investment. By the 1970s, 80 per cent of shipbuilding on the Clyde had vanished.

Although a guarantee of quality, 'Clyde built' also meant the vessel had been constructed through difficult and dangerous manual work. Men worked under some appalling conditions, especially during winter in the open air. Shipyards were veiled in a pall of dusty metal particles and river detritus lapped along the quaysides. The incessant hammering of metal, the arcing of welding torches together with the diabolical tunes played by rivet guns, plying hammers and caulking machines, could all add up to a sense of industrial chaos. Despite the traditional rule of 'measure twice, cut once', many botched jobs found themselves thrown into the Clyde. At one Clyde yard it was said that you could step off a certain quay and walk 20 yards out into the Clyde … and only get your boots wet!

It was a tough existence with little
financial reward. Men worked against time;
dirty gangs in dungarees and bunnets, some
working perilously high up on primitive
staging. Life was tough, with pilfering
accepted by many as normal, especially
when they felt exploited by bosses who
would reduce wages or sack them at the
drop of a hat. Getting material out of yards
and fitting-out basins past gatemen,
commissionaires and security police
demanded considerable ingenuity and
subterfuge, something many workers had in
spades ... it was easier if the gateman was
'in-the-know' and 'winked' you through.
Many Clydeside homes were decorated with
furniture, carpets and fittings from ships being built. A grand
piano from an almost completed vessel once disappeared
overnight. However, small items of intrinsic value, such as brass
plugs for fire hydrants or brass portholes, were the most
popular.

+   +   +

The Jobs

Workforces were divided into three main groups: the 'black
squad', who were mostly pieceworkers carrying out the most
arduous tasks, the hourly-paid finishing trades, and then there
was the staff (from timekeeper to senior management).

Within one trade many people were required. For instance,
in riveting there was a catch-boy, a heater-boy, a puter-in, a
hauder-on, a left-sided riveter and a right-sided riveter; all
operating with a dexterity that would shame a conjuror. The
term 'boy' applied to the job not the person, and many men
were still rivet-boys at retirement. It used to be that squads of
men under one gaffer stayed together over many years. A
budget would be allocated to the gaffer by the shipyard bosses,
and it was up to him to determine the squad size and skills

needed for the job in hand.

For many years riveting was considered one of the top jobs in the yard, as it required physical strength as well as dexterity and skill. A top-class riveter could put in over 600 rivets a day. Riveters worked in gangs, paid for each piece of work according to an agreed price list. The highest prices would be paid for heavy dangerous work. It was not a simple job. First, the rivet-boy took the rivet out of the brazier when it was white-hot. If the rivet cooled before it was totally slaved in and flush, then a burner had to heat it up again. The rivet gun itself was extremely heavy, functioning like a gun that fired a steel bullet which hit a die and made the die jump out.

Ultimately welding took over from riveting as a key requirement in the bonding of steel plates. As a result welders then held considerable bargaining power. Both welders and riveters, along with caulkers, platers, blacksmiths, angle-iron smiths, sheet iron workers, coppersmiths, shipwrights, loftsmen and burners comprised the 'black squad', the workers who were literally at the cutting edge of the process, putting together the structure of the vessel.

Then there were all the finishing trades like plumbers, engineers, electricians, joiners, carpenters, riggers, upholsterers and painters. In the engine shops there were turners, fitters, engineers and brass finishers. In the boiler shops were platers, welders, pressers, boilermakers and caulkers. There was also a host of other skill groups involved in the shipyard including timekeepers, wage clerks, draughtsmen, tracers, gatekeepers, piecework clerks, storemen, labourers, stagers, blacksmiths, liner-offers, crane drivers and French polishers.

The women in the yards were mostly French polishers, tracers, upholsterers, painters or office workers, though some became assistants to the drillers and caulkers, rivet heaters, holders-on or crane drivers, particularly during World War II when the men were on active service or at sea. They soon realised that for them to survive in an environment where men felt free to say the most outrageous and often sexual remarks, they had to be more than up to the task. Some became more forthright and outspoken than the men. Until the 1960s, women who married were expected to leave employment.

Apprentices made up quite a portion of the workforce. The usual rule was that for every apprentice in the yard there had to be four journeymen. And of course there were some weird initiation ceremonies for new apprentices, administered by the men or apprentices themselves. To become a 'time-served' craftsman was to achieve a privileged status, not just within the yard but in the Clydeside community. It was a condition of entry to various exclusive craft unions. An apprenticeship was the process whereby traditional skills and craftsmanship were transmitted from one generation to the next. Unfortunately many apprentices were used as dogsbodies and 'gofers' (ie 'go for'), running here, there and everywhere, especially in the first couple of years of their five-year apprenticeship. Sadly, after their apprenticeship, many were paid off. It is interesting to note that as early as the 1930s apprentices took strike action, when over 12,800 apprentices came out on the Clyde. In 1957 a major apprentices' strike also hit the Clyde.

+   +   +

The Bowler Hats!

Before the introduction of safety helmets, the management were conspicuous around the yard by the bowler hats they wore, many allegedly reinforced in case someone dropped a rivet or half-inch bolt from on high, deliberately or otherwise. There were different levels of management, with yard managers, engineering managers, boiler shop managers and various departmental managers. Then there were foremen, underforemen and chargehands. In many of the sheds the foreman was located in an office or 'wee howff'.

Abuse of power was common, with wages being docked or reduced at a whim. One manager boasted that he always fired the first workman he saw each afternoon after he returned from his liquid lunch. Suspicion and distrust of management permeated many workers' attitudes.

For years the brewing up of tea was prohibited as the workers were deemed to be 'drinking in the firm's time'. Despite

a.m.

the attention of management many unorthodox methods of 'brewing-up' existed. Usually lookouts were posted to keep an eye open for the gaffer. Time was closely controlled as pay was subject to 'quartering' if workers failed to meet starting times, ie 15 minutes deducted from all earnings, including overtime. Only two 'quarters' were allowed in the week.

But it was an amazing sight at the end of the working day, when the horn blew and the yard gates opened. Traffic could be backed-up for miles in each direction at the exodus, careering forward in a mad rush to get home ... away from the 'Bowler Hats'!

✚   ✚   ✚

Health and Safety – 'Who are ye Kiddin', Pal?'

There were very few health and safety regulations in the early days. Accident rates were frighteningly high and fatalities happened regularly in the pandemonium of activity. Once a ship's hull was pretty well on and the scaffolding high up, the wind off the river caused many an accident on slippery planks. And down below, in the confined spaces where it was almost

p.m.

impossible to extract the fumes from the workplace, many
workers succumbed.

If a welder without any eye protection was unlucky enough
to catch sight of a weld being started, the resultant condition
was known as a 'flash'. The condition could last for days with
the unfortunate man unable to open his eyes as he struggled
with the incessant pain described as having sand in your eyes.
Getting caught in machinery was also common. Crane slings
would often break and a steel plate would come hurtling down
to clatter amongst the workers. As bevvying was common in the
yards, workers who went around in an alcoholic bubble were
particularly vulnerable. Little or no protective gear was
provided and for the main part, most workers merely wore their
everyday clothes, dungarees, boots and bunnets, giving an
overall impression of grime and squalor. Some looked like
walking rag-bags.

Yet it is interesting to note that in the earlier part of the
20th century it was possible to determine various skills by their
clothing. A shipwright wore a monkey-jacket and the top button
had to be of brass. A riveter had dark moleskin trousers with
straps round the knees. A joiner might wear a stiff collar
without a tie.

Some yards operated a mutual aid scheme with workers

having sixpence deducted from their pay each week to supplement sickness benefit when required. Bereaved families received a grant of £50 from a death benefit fund administered by a shipyard committee.

In later life many workers were to develop complaints such as asbestosis from the inhalation of asbestos dust. The various processes which involved inhalation of fumes were to cause many chest complaints. Caulkers and riveters were impacted by the constant vibration of their pneumatic drills, chisels and guns and developed what came to be known as 'white finger'. Most workers also developed industrial deafness early on in their shipyard life.

The Clyde's worst shipbuilding disaster happened in 1883 when the steam coaster *Daphne* capsized minutes after launching from Stephen's Govan yard. Two hundred men and boys were finishing off the interior as she was launched – 146 were drowned and it was three weeks before the ship could be raised and the last of the bodies removed. From then onwards only essential personnel were allowed on any ship being launched.

+ + +

'Shitterooteries and the Likes!'

Lack of cleanliness and sanitation caused many an outbreak within the shipyard community. Men went home filthy to places that did not contain a bathroom. Most just stripped to the waist at a kitchen sink to try and wash off the day's dirt. If they were lucky they got a 'dook' in a zinc bath once a week.

Yard toilets were primitive with stale, decaying air mixing with urine and the smell of the great unwashed. Getting off a boat which was well-on in its construction to visit a toilet some distance away was impractical, especially if you were a key member of a squad. Also if away for a long time, you were liable

to have money docked from your pay. So local 'arrangements' on the vessel were made. Pump sumps quickly filled with urine, a particularly foul smell on a warm day. In some yards a 'shit-hoose' clerk existed to monitor workers in and out of the toilet. Some toilets had no light, just sufficient to let a little daylight in. Management did not want workers to sit reading newspapers. Some of the cubicles were nothing more than cut-out holes on a board, with a trough of water flowing underneath. In the early days some yards had toilets built at the end of a quay over the Clyde. 'Deposits' went directly into the river. These facilities were referred to as 'shitterooteries'.

Rats were also a problem in shipyards. Most yards had a rat catcher, though they were always suspected of killing mostly male rats so that they would never be out of work. Yard cats were encouraged as they also helped to keep the rat population under control, but sometimes the rats grew so big and ferocious that they could kill the cats.

+ + +

The Unions

Over 40 separate trade unions represented the men and women involved in the building of a ship.

As methods of production improved and evolved with the introduction of new technologies, there was much antagonism when a particular job was allocated to a trade that had hitherto not been responsible for that particular piece of work. As a result, the number of petty demarcation disputes increased. A major strike once took place because an individual of the 'wrong' union, trying to be helpful, 'pinged' a chalked marking string that lay across a plate to be cut.

A common moan throughout the industry was that the boilermakers, mostly comprised of riveters, platers, caulkers and welders, were usually paid about 50 per cent more than the finishing trades, like plumbers, joiners and engineers. Nevertheless, it was a fact that, however management/union wage negotiations might go, the 'base rate' of the whole industry would stand or fall on the position of the boilermakers, with everyone else's eventual remuneration being merely differentials based upon their rate. When electric welding was introduced in the late 1930s, differences arose between platers and shipwrights as plates were then cut by oxyacetylene torch instead of the guillotine.

✦   ✦   ✦

Launches

Launch days were major celebrations. Here with the birth of a massive structure of thousands of tons came the culmination of many months of work, although she still had to be totally fitted out. Everyone involved in her construction felt great pride as they saw the product of their labours slip into the water.

The ship's owners as well as a range of VIPs and dignitaries were always invited to the event. Flags and bunting adorned the ship and a local band would play. Most ships were launched by women, perhaps the wife or daughter of the ship's owner, or sometimes royalty. A few chosen words were spoken, then a mallet would fall to release the catch holding the locking device or trigger mechanism. The traditional bottle of champagne would smash against the bow with some force, perhaps using a trebuchet arm, and the foreman carpenter would have the holding 'dagger' removed by winch from the great blocks of wood, the 'standing ways' and 'sliding ways', down which the ship would slide into the water. On top of the 'sliding ways' the launch cradle supported the curved sides of the hull. Ever so slowly, the vessel

would commence its journey past groaning timbers and clouds of dust. Massive chains, uncoiling from the clumps they had lain in, acted as drags to ensure that her speed was controlled.

I SAID 'LUNCH' NOT 'LAUNCH'!

After the ceremony the launch party would adjourn to a suitably prestigious establishment where the very best of food and drink was provided by yard management in an effort to entice the ship's owners to give them further orders. However, launches for the tradesmen involved could be bitter-sweet, for often, where there was no further work to fill the berth now vacated, they might be laid-off.

+   +   +

At Home

Unfortunately many men, much to the distress of their families, drank most of their wages after a hard week spent in somewhat appalling conditions. In the early days, foremen paid out the wages in the pub, which more-or-less obliged every man who wished continuing employment, to stand his superior a drink. This practice lead to a pub culture for many.

Shipbuilding was not just about the construction of vessels. It was more than that. Clustered around the banks of the Clyde are many communities who continually felt the chill winds of industrial change and the social distress it brought. When work was plentiful bare floors were covered with wax-cloth and linoleum. When work dried up or disputes dragged on, children might be lucky to have tea and bread for their main daily meal. A common notice held by those outside a shipyard on strike, or during a period of 'lock-out' by management, was 'Idle Cranes Mean Hungry Weans'.

Most workers lived in tenements. Some felt superior on the basis that they lived up a 'wally' or half-tiled 'wally' close whose stairs were religiously covered in pipe-clay by the tenants. Apart from the tiles in the closeway these 'posh' tenements tended to have inside toilets. However most shipyard workers living in tenements had to make do with a toilet on the 'stair-heid' landing. This toilet would be shared with other families, possibly up to four. Chapping on the toilet door to let a neighbour know you were waiting was common. The toilet itself would consist of a well-worn wooden seat and a cistern high above, operated by a chain or perhaps just a piece of string. The inside face of the door usually had carvings or writings by bored occupants. There was no light or heating and a visit during the night, when the only light was the gas mantle on the stair-head, could be daunting. Toilet paper was squares of newspaper cut up. It was said that some families only took the *Glasgow Herald* to show off to their neighbours.

Bathrooms were rare. However in a number of districts public slipper baths were available and well used by shipyard workers. These consisted of rows of narrow compartments, smelling of carbolic, with a duckboard on a cement floor and perhaps a wooden stool beside the bath. A long-handled back-brush and hand-brush made of stiff bristles were also supplied.

During times of no work the pawn shops on Clydeside did good trade. The three golden balls hanging from a wrought-iron bracket were familiar sights. The windows of pawnshops displayed unredeemed pledges for sale. Blankets, bed-linen, dinner sets, cutlery, wedding rings and watches were standard items. Pawnshops were bastions of hope against hunger and poverty in times of strikes and management 'lock-outs'. Still, people did not like to be seen entering a pawnshop. They would trudge to one some distance away from their home or else look in the window of their local pawnshop, as if examining unredeemed pledges, before nonchalantly entering ostensibly to purchase an item. The fact that they left the establishment without the parcel they entered with was usually a clear give-away. Items could be redeemed within a set timeframe, with

interest. Some people sold the pawn ticket for a very small
amount to gain further funds.

Rag stores, where wool or woollen garments no longer
required could be traded for cash depending on their weight,
also provided small havens of economic relief. Menodges, local
saving and loan systems, helped workers' families buy clothes
and household goods, mostly at high interest rates. Wives would
'take-in' washing to earn a few pennies. Some would also 'take-
in' stairs, washing and pipe-claying other folks' tenement stairs.
The shipyard workers' wives and mothers had dignity and
courage in their sacrifice through times of poverty and
depression, in a constant struggle to raise and maintain the
family unit decently.

✦   ✦   ✦

It was Tough!

The hours that a worker was required to work were long and
the conditions under which they worked could be filthy and
dismal. In the early years 50 hours was the working week,
mostly from six in the morning until half-past-five in the
evening, with two breaks of three quarters of an hour for
breakfast and lunch. Eventually this was reduced to 48 hours.
Agreements were reached between various shipyard manage-
ments on starting and stopping times in order to prevent
massive congestion outside yard gates. Then there was the weary
trudge home, dirty boots tramping on pavements, tarnished tea
cans dangling from a satchel, which also contained an empty
medicine bottle used for milk.

There were no official tea breaks. Canteens were almost
unknown. Holiday pay did not exist.

The rules of working were strict. No bevvying was allowed,
though this went on. Workers were not allowed to leave the yard
before the final whistle, and then only through the main gates.
There was to be no pilfering (though the poor wages encouraged
some to do so).

Men used harsh, strong language. Somehow it seemed
appropriate in the environment. Much of it was sexual, religious

or associated with the fitba'. Wicked obscenities were continually exchanged, indeed expected. Sectarian slogans were chalked on plates and discrimination on religious grounds, unfortunately, a reality. But this cast of characters also revelled in wicked humour, piss-taking, slick banter, 'cairry-oans', 'kid-oans' and pranks.

Football was always played in the yards at lunchtime. Many of the matches were 20-a-side affairs with some of the players sporting steel toe-capped boots. The traditional rivalries of the West of Scotland could be displayed in this enthusiastic release from the working routine. Over the years, as conditions gradually improved within the yards and social change proceeded apace, many recreational clubs were created for interested workers, mostly set up by the workforce themselves.

Most Clydeside workers may no longer work in shipbuilding, but there is still the romance, the wonderful history and pride in the great ships produced. See the Clyde ... it flows through your veins and into your dreams. And see shipyard humour, it's legendary!

2

The History of the Clyde Yards

Who knows? Perhaps Noah wasn't the first shipbuilder. Poseidon, Greek God of the Sea, certainly looked kindly on Scotland, for are we not blessed with a long coastline with numerous rivers and sea lochs and islands? It was logical that boats be built as a convenient method of transport, even way back in the mists of time. Certainly in the Clyde area there is much evidence of prehistoric canoes and boats. Much later, in 1329, King Robert the Bruce established a Royal dockyard at Dumbarton.

The Clyde is Scotland's principal river, 106 miles long, rising in the rolling Lowther hills in the Southern Uplands and flowing generally to the north-west by Lanark, through Glasgow, and then westward to the Firth of Clyde. Its story is one of transformation from a shallow meandering river into a vital link with the world's oceans through shipbuilding and trade.

In the 17th century Scottish merchants were keen to develop trade with America and parts of Europe. Herring, salt and linen goods could be traded in France for brandy; tobacco and rum came from America. This led to the dredging of the Clyde as it was unsuitable for any form of further commercial development and initially this was carried out by men using drag chains, with limited success. In 1768 a survey of the Clyde showed a maximum depth of two feet at Kilpatrick. It was proposed that in order to deepen the river 117 jetties should be built out from the river banks, at varying distances apart, so causing the channel to scour itself deeper. After this was done, vessels drawing more than six feet were able to sail to the

Broomielaw at high tide. By 1847 the river depth at the Broomielaw had increased to 18 feet at high tide and 9 feet at low tide.

The building of ships and the many supporting trades and suppliers provided a major opportunity for employment, especially in a country renowned for its inventiveness, its creativity, and its engineering skills. Despite this, shipbuilding on the Clyde has had a chequered history.

After the Act of Union in 1707, Glasgow became the major centre in Europe for importing tobacco from America. However until the American War of Independence (1776-83) most of the ships used by Scotland's tobacco merchants were built in America because of the plentiful supply of North American timber. The war prevented the Scottish merchants from buying

new ships in the Americas and so they
turned to the relatively new but now
flourishing Scottish shipbuilding
industry, primarily on the lower Clyde
at Greenock, Port Glasgow and
Dumbarton. This was essential as
cotton and sugar had also become
important trading commodities.

S S Comet

Shipyards were established on the lower Clyde by men like John
Scott at Greenock, who formed his company in 1711. A yard
was also formed in Ayrshire at Saltcoats, by the Ritchie
brothers. Initially these shipyards built small vessels for
Scottish coastal waters, but eventually progressed to ocean-
going ships.

Then, after Greenock's James Watt's development of the
steam engine in 1769 when steam was first condensed outside the
cylinder, engineers experimented with the use of steam engines
for the propulsion of ships. These smaller, more powerful,
engines required less coal than the earlier types. The first
commercially viable ship that regularly traded and was
propelled by steam was the SS *Comet*, her name inspired by a
sighting of Halley's Comet in the west of Scotland the previous
year. She was built through the visionary enthusiasm of Henry
Bell of Helensburgh in 1812, during the Napoleonic wars. Lord
Nelson supported Bell's view but the mainstream of opinion was
hostile to the use of steam. Its internal flue boiler was built in
Glasgow by Robertson and company, whilst her hull was
produced on the Lower Clyde. *Comet* was about 40 feet in
length and fitted with a 4hp engine driving at first two pairs of
paddles, but ultimately one.

She ran between Glasgow, Greenock and Helensburgh
carrying passengers only. It took her four hours to steam the
distance from Glasgow to Greenock, a trip that had previously
taken over a day by oar and sail. Unfortunately fuel
consumption was excessive and therefore her sailing range was
limited. It was said that on her maiden voyage the passengers
had to wade in the water on one occasion and push her off after
grounding. It is rumoured that two male passengers
disembarked at Bowling fearing what they thought would be an

inevitable boiler explosion. An exact replica of the *Comet* exists outside Port Glasgow Town Hall, very close to its birthplace at John Wood's shipyard. It is a poignant reminder of the exciting early days of steam.

From 1812 to 1820, some 42 steam ships were built on the river, mostly by Scott's of Greenock and William Denny at Dumbarton. They proved that steamboats could be much faster and more reliable than horse-drawn or sailing ships. However there was concern that a ship driven by steam would be unable to cross the Atlantic due to the immense consumption of coal required with the result that there would be little room left for cargo.

From 1820 onwards many shipbuilders elsewhere throughout the UK copied, and in many instances, improved on, Henry Bell's models. At this time ships made of iron were being slowly introduced, with the first iron shipyard on the Clyde created in 1834, by Tod and MacGregor at the mouth of the River Kelvin. Scotland was lucky. The country had iron ore and the coal with which to extract the iron, nearby in Lanarkshire.

In 1841, the influential marine engineer, Robert Napier, opened a shipyard at Govan to produce iron-built steamships. This yard is generally acknowledged to be the 'cradle of modern shipbuilding' on the Clyde. Up until his death in 1876, Napier was to prove to be a major influence on shipbuilding and one of the main entrepreneurs in the establishment and development of shipbuilding on the Clyde. He is now fondly remembered as the 'Father of Clyde Shipbuilding'. In 1843 his first iron ship, PS *Vanguard*, was launched. The cost of producing an iron ship was much dearer than a wooden one, but the running costs were found to be substantially lower. By the 1860s he was established both at home and abroad as a shipbuilder, marine engineer and financier of great repute. Robert Napier's insistence on work of the highest quality provided an excellent training ground in the new techniques. His trainees, like John Elder, went on to develop the compound engine and, in turn, Alexander Kirk produced the triple-expansion engine which had such a major and long-lasting impact on marine propulsion.

The building of tea-clippers became popular in the mid-

1800s. These brigs were mostly built
for the West India trade. The vessels
used an iron frame combined with a
wooden planked hull fixed to the
frame by metal bolts. In 1866 'the
Great Tea Race' took place when two
Clyde-built ships competed. After

The Clipper 'Ariel'

travelling from China in 99 days the *Ariel* and the *Taiping*
arrived 10 minutes apart in the English channel. The tea clipper
boom lasted until the beginning of the 1870s when the opening of
the Suez canal brought an end to the demand for this type of
ship.

The further development of the triple-expansion engine in
the 1880s, saw the emergence of the express luxury liner to meet
the needs of rival shipping lines on the North Atlantic run. They
had a new profile: clipper bows became straight stems and
deckhouses were consolidated into one superstructure. Masts
still carried enough sail to provide back-up should the engines
fail, but engines were becoming more and more reliable. Then in
1893 the Cunard ships, *Campania* and *Lucania*, built by
Fairfields, entered the North Atlantic scene. Truly luxurious,
they were capable of over 23 knots.

Next came the steam turbine, replacing reciprocating
machinery to propel huge liners. The size and tonnage of ships
suddenly increased: the *Lusitania* was built by John Brown's in
1906 and was the first vessel over 30,000 tons – she was capable
of exceeding 26 knots. These superliners were to became ever
more luxurious over the years.

The Clyde grew in importance not just for shipbuilding but
as a trading area. Wharfs and docks were established near
Glasgow and shipbuilding
yards relocated down-
river. Thomson's yard at
Govan moved to
Clydebank and
ultimately became John
Brown's – the original
Govan site becoming
Princes Dock. Barclay

R M S Lusitania

Aquitania

Curle moved from Stobcross to Whiteinch and Alexander Stephen from Kelvinhaugh to Linthouse for the new Queen's Dock. These moves enabled the shipyards to be bigger and better equipped to build the ever-increasing demand for larger vessels.

In the early part of the 20th century, the lower Clyde, flowing through the heart of Clydeside, had become the industrial heart of Scotland. From the centre of Glasgow to Clydebank and beyond, either riverbank was now occupied with docks, shipyards and engine shops. Thus the conditions were set for the Clyde to become the most famous shipbuilding river in the world. By the start of World War I the Clyde had virtually reached the maximum number of shipyards possible. At that time there were a total of 38 shipyards from Greenock to Glasgow, building vessels from tugs to massive liners.

Warship construction took up a significant portion of the Clyde's output. Way back in the days of sail the British Admiralty built almost all of its own warships in Government yards, but by the time of the German/British naval race preceding World War I, it was mostly private shipbuilders that were building Britain's fleet of warships.

One of the first huge warships was the iron ship *Black Prince* built by Robert Napier at Govan. At the start of the 20th century the number of orders from the Admiralty dramatically increased with the rapidly deteriorating international situation. Prior to the start of war in 1914 there were five prime yards on the Clyde associated with building warships: Beardmore at Dalmuir, Brown's at Clydebank, Yarrows at Scotstoun, Fairfield in Govan and Scott's of Greenock. Some smaller yards did occasionally obtain Admiralty orders.

Order books fluctuated over the years. As it was difficult to always obtain continuity of orders most workers were employed on a casual basis (perhaps slipping the foreman of a squad a half-crown in the pub), and of course workers could be dismissed without notice. Many of the owners proved unscrupulous and this, together with the poor conditions of employment, understandably resulted in an extreme militancy in many yards. Demarcation disputes between trades abounded. Communist and extreme socialist views prevailed, with the result that the term, 'Red Clydeside' was often used.

It was common for squads carrying out various tasks in the yard to be laid off once their part of the building of a ship was complete, or shortly after the launch. Many men refused to change from the trade they had learned, defending their right to that particular skill regardless of its overall implications. For this reason the shipbuilding industry was continually dogged by demarcation disputes. Woe betide the fellow who did more than was expected of him, even when he was trying to be helpful. Time was lost waiting for a person from a particular union to come and finish even a simple task.

In the early 1900s the number of workers involved in shipbuilding on the Clyde was estimated at more than 100,000 and four times as many workers were involved in supply businesses to the shipbuilding industry.

Unfortunately, after World War I, a series of treaties were signed between Britain and Germany limiting naval tonnage. This, together with the depression of the 1920s, had a major impact on the Clyde. The Clyde did not hit boom times again until the years proceeding World War II and many yards disappeared as they either closed or were absorbed by other firms.

29

The 1930s brought a virtual halt to shipbuilding on the Clyde and silence fell over the great yards. In December 1930 the keel was laid at John Brown's of Clydebank for an 80,000-ton liner, number '534'. Work progressed for a year until the depression forced the suspension of the contract with Cunard. Just before Christmas 1931 the shipyard laid off some 3,000 workers with up to 10,000 others in sub-contracted work also losing their jobs.

Cunard approached the Government of the day to ask for a

Queen Elizabeth

Queen Mary

subsidy to finish this liner, *Queen Mary*, plus a sister ship *Queen Elizabeth*. The Government agreed, provided Cunard also agreed to a merger with the White Star Line, which was also in financial difficulty. An agreement was reached between the two companies and work restarted on the 3rd April 1934. The first job was to remove over 100 tons of rust that had accumulated on the hull of '534'. She was launched in September the same year.

With rearmament World War II saw the yards again working to capacity, bringing much needed relief to the industry. However as the Clyde was the country's principal naval base, port and shipbuilding area, it became a target for enemy bombers. Glasgow, Clydebank and Greenock were the main victims. During the war 37 Clyde shipyards built an amazing 1,903 vessels, converted 637 and repaired more than 25,000. Also fabricated were over 30,000 tons of sections of Mulberry floating harbours for the Normandy invasion. After the war there was a mini-boom in shipbuilding, primarily replacing vessels lost in the conflict. Unfortunately recession set in once more in the mid-1950s, exacerbated by union and management problems over manning levels, hours, conditions and levels of productivity. Competition between yards for orders was cut-throat. From time to time many quotes for ships were submitted which were loss-making. Yards might also occasionally build a ship 'on spec', hoping that they would be able to sell her later.

The Clyde gradually started to lose its dominant position in world shipbuilding. Yards in Korea, Japan, Norway and Germany, using modern prefabrication methods, and without the impact of regular industrial relations problems, were proving successful. (It also

Oxfordshire

has to be said that the industry was subsidised in some countries, either directly or indirectly.) The contraction of the British Empire's economic capacity was another major factor.

The modernisation of yards and better relationships with workforces came too late. Delivery dates slipped and technical problems became prevalent. Many skilled workers emigrated to find work. The work-in at Upper Clyde Shipbuilders in 1971, when workers responded to the need to save the yard, proved successful but only for while.

Today only the BAe System's yards at Scotstoun and Govan are left, together with Ferguson's yard at Port Glasgow. Sadly neglected dock areas remain and there is little activity on the river. The future remains uncertain, but the River Clyde continues to flow thereby giving the opportunity to future entrepreneurs, if the economic climate is right, to restore our shipbuilding heritage ... after all, 95 per cent of trade throughout the world is still carried by sea.

But the real pride of the Clyde is, of course, its people. They, like the river, are still here.

+   +   +

Clydeside Yards and Marine Engine Works – 1960

Ailsa Shipbuilding and Eng. Co. Ltd.,
    Troon Shipyard and Eng. Works.
Ardrossan Dockyard Co. Ltd., Ardrossan Shipyard.
Blythswood Shipbuilding Co. Ltd., Scotstoun Shipyard.
John Brown and Co. (Clydebank) Ltd.
Wm. Denny and Bros. Ltd., Dumbarton Engine Works.
Wm. Denny and Bros. Ltd., Leven Shipyard, Dumbarton.
Barclay Curle and Co. Ltd., Elderslie Dry Docks.
Barclay Curle and Co. Ltd., Clydeholm Shipyard.
Barclay Curle and Co. Ltd., North British Engine Works.
Chas. Connell and Co. Ltd., Scotstoun Shipyard.
D & W Henderson, Meadowside Dry Dock and Repair Quay.
A & J Inglis Ltd., Pointhouse Shipyard.
David Rowan and Co. Ltd., Finnieston Engine Works.

Harland and Wolff Ltd., Govan Shipyard.

Harland and Wolff Ltd., Finnieston Engine Works.

British Polar Engines Ltd., Govan Engine Works.

Fairfield Shipbuilding and Eng. Co. Ltd.,
     Govan Shipyard and Engine Works.

Alexander Stephen and Sons Ltd., Linthouse Shipyard
     and Engineering Works.

Scott and Sons Ltd., Bowling Shipyard.

Wm. Simons and Co. Ltd., Renfrew Shipyard
     and Engine Works.

Lobnitz and Co. Ltd., Renfrew Shipyard and Engine Works.

Fleming and Ferguson Ltd., Phoenix Shipyard
     and Engine Works, Paisley.

Lamonts, Castle Shipyard, Port Glasgow.

Ferguson Bros. Ltd., Newark Shipyard, Port Glasgow.

Lithgows Ltd., East Yard, Port Glasgow.

Lithgows Ltd., Kingston Yard, Port Glasgow.

Yarrow and Co. Ltd., Scotstoun Shipyard and Engine Works.

Wm. Hamilton and Co. Ltd., Glen Shipyard, Port Glasgow.

Firth of Clyde Drydock Co. Ltd., Inchgreen Drydock,
     Greenock.

George Brown and Co., (Marine) Ltd., Garvel Shipyard,
     Greenock.

Greenock Dockyard Co. Ltd., Cartsdyke Shipyard, Greenock.

Hastie's Ltd, Greenock.

John G. Kincaid and Co. Ltd., Greenock Engine Works.

Scotts Shipbuilding and Eng. Co. Ltd.,
     Cartsburn Shipyard, Greenock.

Scotts Shipbuilding and Eng. Co. Ltd.,
     Greenock Engine Works.

3

Some interesting Clyde-built ships

Livadia

In 1879 John Elder and company of Govan built a ship, the *Livadia*, for the Tsar Alexander. Its unique specifications were provided by Russia's chief naval designer. The ship was to be 230 feet long, 152 feet wide at its broadest point and the draught only 6 feet. The tonnage was 7,200. It was to be a 'water palace'.

Although John Elder and Company had major misgivings at such specifications the order was taken, and the ship duly launched in July 1880. The ship was fitted out with luxurious staterooms. In September 1880 it sailed to London where the Grand Duke Alexis, the Tsar's son, boarded with a retinue of aristocratic guests and servants. Its maiden voyage was to be to the Crimean sea port, Sevastopol, on the Black Sea. Six weeks later the ship arrived in Fuengirola in Spain. It transpired that in the Bay of Biscay the ship had been tossed about, completely out of control with the crew and passengers soaked and weary with seasickness. A week later the voyage recommenced but the design of the ship caused mayhem every time the wind got up. Eventually the ship reached Sevastopol. The Tsar never saw his 'floating palace' as he was assassinated and the *Livadia* never put to sea again. Her three engines and luxury fittings were stripped out and she was broken up in 1927.

+ + +

The QE2
The last Great Trans-Atlantic
Liner to be Built on the Clyde

The task of building a new Queen, following *Queen Mary* and the *Queen Elizabeth*, was given to John Brown and Company of Clydebank. The company had also built the *Lusitania* and the Royal Yacht *Britannia*, as well as hundreds of other prestigious vessels.

The contract for the new Queen was signed on the 30th December 1964. On the 5th July 1965, the keel was laid on the same slipway that had held the *Queen Mary*. The new Queen was known as 'John Brown Hull 736' because, like the *Queen Mary*, this new ship would not get a name until the day of her launch, the owners having codenamed her Q4 until then. The Cunard White Star Line considered a number of names for their new liner. 'Winston Churchill', 'William Shakespeare', 'Great Britain', 'London', 'Queen Mary 2', 'Mauritania' and 'Britannia' were amongst the many names put forward. Finally the decision was made to call her *Queen Elizabeth 2*.

On the 20th September 1967, just 27 months after the keel was laid, *Queen Elizabeth 2* was launched and christened by Her Majesty Queen Elizabeth the Second. Using the same golden scissors as her mother and grandmother had used to launch previous Queens, Her Majesty, beside Prince Phillip, Princess Margaret and Cunard Chairman Sir Basil Smallpiece, cut the ribbon releasing the bottle of champagne against the bow of Cunard's new flagship. The trigger mechanism for the launching

was then released and the retaining wedges pulled away,
allowing the great liner's large and gracious hull to begin moving
down the ways. At 2.30pm the ship entered the waters of the
River Clyde to be held in check by the massive launch chains
and lines from the waiting tugs. Tumultuous crowds lined both
shores of the river, with cheering workmen swarming over the
gantries, and a squadron of military aircraft flying overhead in
anchor-formation. The men who had fashioned her had lumps
in their throats – they had built other ships, but this one was
special. From the youngest apprentice to the yard directors they
had all played their part in shaping this sterling liner. For the
rest of their lives they would fervently follow her career.

Once she was floating happily beside the fitting-out dock,
the tugs, released from their task, chugged proudly back to
their berths. The fitting-out work then proceeded apace on this
new flagship for Cunard. She was immediately perceived as
different from the previous Cunarders as she had only one
funnel. Also it had been decided that the funnel would be
painted white instead of the hitherto famous orange and black
colours. On the 19th of November the ship was moved to dry
dock in Greenock, some 18 miles down the Clyde from her place
of birth, before beginning sailing trials.

In November 1968, the *QE2* went on sea trials which
unfortunately went rather badly. She suffered from technical
problems with her turbines and was forced to return. However
in April 1969, the *QE2* joined the Cunard fleet for transatlantic
crossings. She left Southampton for New York on her maiden
voyage on the 2nd of May. The American interest in the new
Queen proved enormous and her first summer of service highly
profitable.

The first dramatic incident of note in the *QE2*'s service
occurred in January 1971. Whilst cruising in the Caribbean a
SOS call was received from the French liner *Antilles*. It had run
aground near Mustique and leaking fuel had caught fire inside
the ship. By the time the *QE2* arrived the *Antilles* was an
inferno. The passengers, who had already been taken ashore to
Mustique in lifeboats, then boarded the *QE2* and two French
ships which had arrived to assist before being landed in
Barbados. The *Antilles* eventually capsized and sank.

On the 17th May 1972 whilst travelling from New York to Southampton, a message was received by the *QE2*'s Captain that there was a bomb on board, timed to go off during the voyage. A search by the crew found nothing and so a bomb disposal unit was flown out and parachuted into the sea near to the ship. The incident proved to be a hoax and the FBI arrested the hoaxer.

Then in 1973 terrorists threatened to blow her up as she steamed towards Israel.

Despite major competition from the airlines, the *QE2* continued to attract passengers and in 1975 Cunard opted to send their magnificent flagship on her first world cruise. The QE2 has an advantage over many cruise ships as she was built for Atlantic weather rather than sheltered warm waters. She has a strong hull and the matching power to ignore gales, punch through hurricanes and so is able to withstand weather which sends other ships fleeing for shelter.

In 1982 with the Falklands war looming, the Admiralty requisitioned two liners, the *QE2* and P&O's *Canberra* as troop transport. Helicopter decks and military communications systems were installed on the *QE2* – the 5th Infantry Brigade, made up of the Scots and Welsh Guards together with the Gurkhas, comprised the 'passengers'. Fearing that the *QE2* would prove an attractive target even with her newly painted grey hull, the liner was, on the 12th May 1982, sent to South Georgia, about 1,500 miles from Argentina. There the troops transferred to the *Canberra*. The *QE2* then took on board survivors of *HMS Ardent*, a casualty of the war. At that stage it became known that the Argentinians were using air reconnaissance to try to locate the *QE2*, so she quickly headed north. She arrived back in Southampton on the 11th June and work immediately began to restore her for commercial service. On the 2nd December the same year, the Queen Mother unveiled a plaque onboard commemorating the liner's contribution to the Falklands conflict.

Shortly after her Falklands duty, Cunard opted to repaint the ship's funnel from white to the traditional Cunard colours of orange and black.

In April 1984 the ship suffered minor damage after

colliding with a breakwater at Piraeus, the gateway to Athens. In October the same year an electrical fire caused a complete loss of power and delayed the *QE2* for two days. On her return to Southampton it was decided that diesel engines would have to be fitted in order to increase efficiency. This work was started in October 1986 by Lloyd Werfte, at Bremerhaven in Germany and it was estimated this would save the company some £12m a year in fuel costs. Nine diesel-electric engines were installed and new propellers were fitted along with a new funnel of different design, its stack wider that the old one. By 1987 she was back in service.

On the 7th August 1992, while cruising in the Vineyard Sound off Martha's Vineyard near the coast of Massachusetts, the *QE2* ran aground, damaging parts of the keel and bow. Passengers were evacuated and the liner forced to go into dry dock. What came out of the subsequent investigation was that the speed of the liner had pushed the water away from the massive vessel and had literally dug a hole in the water, thereby grounding her on uncharted rocks.

On the 11th September 1995 on a west-bound crossing, the ship encountered Hurricane Luis and was hit by a 95-foot wave. This caused the ship to arrive late into New York and delayed her for a day whilst repairs were effected.

In 1994, 1996 and 1999 further extensive refits were carried out, with interiors being refurbished to meet modern cruising standards. The *QE2* now looks somewhat different than she did over 30 years ago. There is more space at the aft end and many changes have been made to her interior, including the Yacht Club Room and the Queen's Grill.

On the 29th August 2002 a historic moment was reached: the *QE2* had logged 5 million miles at sea – a proud day for the men who had built her and a testimony to their skills.

The *QE2* Specifications:
Yard Number: 736
Shipbuilder: John Brown, Clydebank
Propulsion: originally steam turbine then diesel electric
Length: 963 feet (294m)
Beam: 105 feet (32m)

Tonnage: 70,327 gross tons (originally 65,863 gross tons)
Deep draught: 32 feet (9.8m)
Service Speed: 32.4 knots (58.5 Km/h)
Passengers: 1,900
Crew: 1,015
Rudder: 75 tons
2 propellers of 22ft diameter, 42 tons
2 bow thrusters

+   +   +

Empress of Britain
1931-40

Canadian Pacific gave Clydebank shipbuilders John Brown and
Co the task of building their latest flagship. Canadian Pacific
were already into the cruising business but the company wanted
their new ship to be dual-purpose. She was to operate as an
Atlantic liner in the summer season and to go on long cruises in
the winter. So the *Empress of Britain*, one of three vessels which
have been so named, was built with luxury in mind. Her main
feature was the Mayfair lounge, beautifully furnished in walnut
and complemented with silver panelling. There was also a large
gymnasium for those passengers trying to work off the legacy of

the liner's culinary delights.

Her launch day was June the 11th 1930 and the actual christening was carried out by a man, Edward, Prince of Wales. The liner was fitted with Curtis-Brown steam turbines geared to four propellers, providing a service speed of 24 knots. However during her sea trials on the measured mile off Arran she attained 25.27 knots, much to the delight of her new owners.

On May 27th 1931 the *Empress of Britain* set out on her maiden voyage from Southampton to Quebec, calling at Cherbourg en route. Her time from Cherbourg to Father Point was 4 days, 19 hours and 35 minutes, the fastest ever crossing. On the 3rd December 1931 she set off on her first world cruise. As speed was not important on this leisure cruise, two of her turbines were shut down and her two outer propellers removed and stowed aboard to reduce drag, thereby cutting down fuel consumption.

In June 1935 she was involved in her first major accident. This happened in fog when she collided with the *Kafiristan*, and three people on board this vessel were killed.

In June 1939 King George VI and Queen Elizabeth completed their goodwill tour of North America by chartering the *Empress of Britain* for their return trip. However on the 25th of September the ship was requisitioned as a troop carrier with the commencement of hostilities in World War II. She then made two crossings carrying troops between Halifax, Nova Scotia and the Clyde. In March 1940 the liner was sent to Australia and New Zealand to transport troops to Europe.

In the autumn of 1940, the *Empress of Britain* was on a trooping mission between England and Suez via the Cape. On October 26th, with 643 people on board, the ship was suddenly attacked by a German long-range Focke-Wulf Condor plane. The *Empress* was set on fire and the captain ordered abandon ship, although a skeleton crew remained onboard in an effort to save her. The Polish destroyer *Burza* and two tugs managed to take the burning liner in tow, but the German aircraft had reported the ship's position. Soon the German U-boat, *U-32*, began stalking the crippled liner. The torpedoes fired by the U-boat struck home and the *Empress of Britain* went down with the loss of 49 souls. Two days later *U-32* was sunk by the destroyer *Harvester*.

The *Empress of Britain* Specifications:
Length: 760.6 feet (231.84 m)
Beam: 97.8 feet (9.79 m)
Tonnage: 42,348 gross tons.
Engines: Four Curtis-Brown steam turbines turning
    four propellers.
Service Speed: 24 knots.
Passengers: 1,195

+ + +

TS King Edward

The world's first commercial steam turbine ship was the TS *King Edward*. She was built at William Denny's Dumbarton shipyard and launched in 1901. Weighing around 550 tons she was built as an experimental vessel for the Turbine Steamer Syndicate. With three direct-drive turbines she proved to be highly efficient and economical, reaching speeds of over 20 knots.

It is interesting to note that she spent most of her working life locally. As a passenger/cruise vessel she sailed around the West coast of Scotland between places such as Campbeltown and Dunoon. During World War I the TS *King Edward* was seconded as a troop ship mostly on the English Channel, then as a hospital ship in the White Sea in the Russian Arctic.

After the war she sailed for William Buchanan Steamers Ltd., between Glasgow and Rothesay, Bute. During World War II she remained working on the Clyde on commercial work associated with the war effort, before returning to passenger cruising in 1946 under the ownership of the Caledonian Steam Packet Co. Ltd.

Just after her 50th year of service she was sold for scrap. However her two turbine engines were removed to the Scottish Maritime Museum at Irvine.

+ + +

The Royal Yacht Britannia

One of the most important factors in the placing of the contract for the construction of the *Britannia* was the requirement that the ship be completed by the end of 1953 or Spring 1954 at the latest. Seven firms competed for the ship's construction and it became obvious that John Brown and Co of Clydebank were best suited to meet the deadline. The order was officially placed with Brown's in February 1952, the keel laid on June 16th 1952, and the vessel launched on April 16th 1953. It was completed and accepted by the Admiralty on 11th January 1954.

The vessel served Queen and country for 44 years, on 968 official voyages throughout all parts of the globe. The *Britannia's* last voyage was to Hong Kong and back, in early 1997. On the 11th December of the same year the *Britannia* was decommissioned at Portsmouth Naval Base in the presence of 16 members of the Royal Family. *Britannia* is now permanently moored in Leith, giving visitors the rare opportunity to get on board a truly royal vessel.

The *Britannia* Specifications:
Overall length: 412ft 3in.
Maximum breadth: 55ft
Gross tonnage: 5,769 tons.
Continuous seagoing speed: 21 knots.
Masts: Three. The Royal Standard at the main, the Flag of the
    Lord High Admiral at the fore, and the Union Flag at
    the mizzen.

4

Remembered in word and song

The Christening

There was a man,
And all his life
He'd worked in a shipyard;
And he had a baby,
And it was going to be christened;
And for a week
He couldn't sleep nights,
Because he was worried
For fear the minister
Would hurt the baby
When he hit it with the bottle.

+   +   +

She's Sailed Awa!

The day she sailed was terrible,
That night he yelled, 'Oh lord!'
But her absence wisnae the problem,
He'd left his screwtap aboard!

+   +   +

Get Yer Ain Back!

If a gaffer won't let ye bile yer can,
Then jist get an orange oot forthwith.
An' when he sees ye scoopin' it oot,
He'll know that yer takin' the pith!

+   +   +

Doon Behind the Yaird Gates

Doon behind the yard gates,
Ah met a man called Fred,
A right-handed riveter,
Till the left wan hit his head.

Doon behind the yaird gates,
A gaffer on the snoop,
Lookin' fur the workers
Oan electric soup.

Doon behind the yaird gates,
Ah saw a bowler hat,
Wid fire ye in a minute,
That old b's a rat!

Doon behind the yaird gates,
Hiding behind a dyke.
Wee shop stewards aw plannin'
Anither bliddy strike.

Doon behind the yaird gates,
A wee man wi' a clock.
Lookin' oot fur late yins,
Their pathetic pay tae dock.

Doon behind the yaird gates,
The cranes patrol o'erhead.
Men an' boys at 'cairry-oans',
In the plating shed.

+   +   +

East of Suez

Sail me east of Suez,
Where the best are like the worst,
And there ain't no ten commandments,
An' yaird gaffer's fit tae burst!

+   +   +

The Poor Auld Hauder-On

Somebody stole the hobby,
From the poor auld hauder-on
An' noo he's standin' doin' nought,
That poor auld hauder-on

Oh, the poor auld hauder-on,
Oh, the poor auld hauder-on,
Somebody stole the hobby from
The poor auld hauder-on.

Noo that he's nae hobby,
I guess we'll see some fun,
Fur he's gonnae shoot the thief,
Wi' the loan o' a rivet gun!

Note: A hobby was the tool which allowed the 'hauder-on' to
apply leverage to the rivet.

+   +   +

The Song of The Clyde

I sing of a river I'm happy beside,
The song that I sing is the song of the Clyde;
Of all Scottish Rivers it's dearest to me
It flows from Leadhills all the way to the sea.
It borders the orchards of Lanark so fair
Meanders through meadows with sheep grazing there
But from Glasgow to Greenock, in towns on each side
The hammers ding-dong is the song of the Clyde.

Oh the River Clyde, the wonderful Clyde
The name of it thrills me and fills me with pride
And I'm satisfied what e'er may betide
The sweetest of songs is the song of the Clyde.

The shipyards aw fu' o' perspiring men,
Anxious tae run oot the yaird gates again.
Up tae their antics, shindigs an' larks,
A right shower that bunch, jist like welders' arcs.
An' yet fae the nonsense a ship it arose,
Fae rusty auld metal aw cut oot wi' holes,
A miracle built wi' humour an' pride,
Alang on the banks by the side o' the Clyde.

When sun sets on shipyards, there's beauty to see,
The QE2 liner is down by the quay.
The blast o' its horn loudly echoes, and then
A stillness descends on the water again.
Tis' here that the sea-going legend was born,
But, unlike the salmon, it seldom returns.
Can you wonder the Scots o'er the ocean so wide,
Should constantly long for this pride o' the Clyde.

+   +   +

The Yairds
By John Fergus

I've worked amang them, man and boy, for mair than fifty year,
I canna bear to quit them yet noo that I'm auld an' sair.
The Yairds is just the life o' me, the music's in my bluid
O' hammers striking strong an' true on rivets glowing rid;
I'm auld, I ken, but, Goad be thank'd! I hivna lost ma pride
In honest work on bonny boats that's built upon the Clyde.

Frae Broomielaw to Kempoch Point I ken them every yin,
I kent them as a rivet boy, I kent them in ma prime,
An' tho there's been an unco wheen o' changes in ma time,
Yet still it's aye a bonny sicht to see them in their pride,
Wi' ways' laid doon an' some big boat aw ready for the tide.

It's grand to see the boats grow up frae keel to upper strake,
An' ken it's aw guid honest work an' no' an ounce o' fake;
It's grand tae see the muckle frames staun' up like leafless trees,
To hear the clang o' plates an' feel the rivet furnace breeze
To see the bonny boats tak' shape just like a living thing,
Eh, man, but it's a bonny sicht an' fit to please a king.

I've helped to build a wheen o' them in mony a different yaird,
Frae barges up to battleships the Empire for to guard,
An' aye, the names I can reca' o' men noo passed awa,
Wha planned and built the boats lang syne,
    aye trig and strong and braw.
The men hae gone, but left ahint a legacy o' fame,
For honest work and bonny boats that gied the Clyde its name.

Ye'll hear it said the 'Black Squad' drink an'
    break their time forbye,
Weel I jaloose we hae oor faults, just let the jaw gang by;
But this I'll say that, gin we drink an' break oot time as weel,
Wi' aw oor faults, by Goad! We ken hoo to lay a keel,
An' build a boat that nane can bate in aw the world beside,
The best o' work, the bonniest boats aye come
    frae oot the Clyde.

Woe's me!

Woe's me, woe's me,
The acorn's no' yet
Fallen fae the tree.
That's tae grow the wood,
That's tae mak the cradle,
Tae haud the next ship,
If this bliddy strike goes oan much longer!
Aye, woe's me.

5

Shipyard humour!

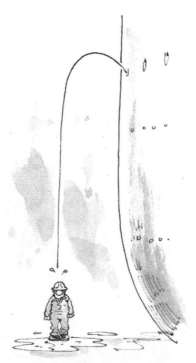

Falling rivets from above or someone urinating over the side of the hull were constant hazards for those working below. One afternoon someone opted to take a 'widdle' from deck level. Sitting directly below the stream of urine was the unfortunate Danny, who had at that very moment decided to remove his bunnet. Danny stood up, soaked and ponging.

His charge-hand passed by and observed. 'Well, Danny boy, at least ye'll get a seat oan the bus tae yersel the night!'

+   +   +

'Excuse me, Jimmy,' asked the stranger in the yard. 'Could ye tell me where ah can find the urinal?'

'Hoo many funnels does she have?'

+ + +

At the lunch break, 'One-eyed Beekie' always laid his flask and pieces on top of his bench. Then he took out his glass eye, and put it down beside his lunch, much to the disgust of his mates.

'Why dae ye take it oot at the lunch break, Beekie?' asked someone.

'It jist keeps an eye oan ma lunch so that nane o' you thieving lot wull pinch it!'

+ + +

Bobbie Ferguson, a pompous wee under-foreman caulker, was promoted to foreman. He assembled his squad around him and let them know, in no uncertain terms, that from now on he was the boss and a man to be reckoned with. 'Furthermore,' he added, 'in future I am Mister Ferguson, and I want to be addressed as such!'

From then on the men called him *Such*!

+ + +

It was mid-morning and a gaffer was called to the gates; someone who had been recommended to him was there looking for a job.

'Ah'm lookin' fur a start,' said the fellow, a cunning look in his eye.

'Whit's yer trade?'

'Och, this an' that.'

'Where have ye worked before?'

'Here an' there. So when dae ah start?'

'Och, sooner or later,' said the gaffer, turning on his heel.

+ + +

The rivet catch-boy fell 15 feet off the staging round the hull and was lucky to escape unscathed. His journeyman climbed down, picked him up and exclaimed, 'Listen, Humpty-Dumpty. Ah thought ah telt ye no' tae scratch yer bum wi' baith hauns at the wan time.'

+   +   +

'Old Jock' was 74, a retired boilermaker. In the yard where he had worked there was a special job on, and his old foreman remembered that Old Jock was the only person who knew exactly where to cut holes in a vital piece of steel, for the engine room of a ship under construction. 'Aye, Old Jock knows that particular wee joab backside furrit,' he observed.

His old foreman duly visited Jock and asked if he would come into the yard to measure the vital plate. He would of course be paid for his trouble.

At the agreed time the old boilermaker duly arrived. After studying the steel plate for a couple of minutes, he carefully measured it before putting cross marks in chalk where the holes should be bored.

A couple of days later the yard got a bill from Old Jock for ten pounds and sixpence. It was sent back to Jock by the invoicing department asking for a breakdown of the cost.

The reply came the following day. It read: 'Cost of chalk: 6 pence. Knowing where to put the marks: £10.'

He was paid!

+   +   +

'Big Eck', a somewhat slow-witted red-leader in the yard, got a splash of red-lead paint in his eye. He staggered off to the timekeeper who also doubled as the first-aid man.

'Sit doon, son,' said the old timekeeper, 'we'll soon hae ye sorted.' He took out an eye-bath and poured some optic solution into it. 'Here ye are, son' he said, putting the brimming eye bath into Big Eck's hand.

'Cheers!' exclaimed Big Eck, and gulped it down.

+   +   +

'See the launch next week,' observed wee Malky peering over his pint. 'Ah think it wid hae been mair appropriate if instead o' the chairman's wife launching the boat, auld Sam wis tae dae it. Efter aw he's been in the yard fur years an' years.'

'Don't be daft, Malky,' replied his drinking companion Shug. 'Auld Sam's a bevvy merchant. He widnae let go o' the bottle!'

+   +   +

'Ah'm no' gonnae work fur that bugger o' a foreman again!' exclaimed Danny.

'Why no'?' enquired Pat

'He's jist given me ma books!'

+   +   +

The thin woman painter happened to walk by a group of apprentices.

'Hey, Mrs Wummin, ah've seen mair meat on a butcher's pencil,' one observed cheekily.

'Aye, an' your wee sausage has goat nae chance!' came the retort.

+   +   +

The apprentice was heating up a can of tea in front of the furnace when he was caught by the gaffer.

'Whose tea is that?' demanded the gaffer.

'Coe's,' replied the wee lad.

'Well, jist you tell Coe that ah want tae see him. This isnae Crawford's Tea Rooms, ye ken!'

Once the gaffer had gone, the wee fella was asked about Coe's tea.

'Co-operative tea!' grinned the lad.

+   +   +

'Ah thought ye wis aff sick yesterday, Smithie?' said his charge-hand.

'Aye, ah wis.'

'Then how come ah hear ye scored a goal fur Clydebank Juniors yesterday efternoon?'

'Well, if ah hudnae o' been sick ah wid probably have goat a hat trick!'

+   +   +

The charge-hand was putting together a squad.

'An' whit dae you dae?' he asked one of the hopefuls.

'Och, ah jist aye live aff ma wits.'

'So you'll be happy tae work fur half-pay, then?'

+   +   +

Dougie was keen on the greyhounds and had two at home. One day he arrived back at the family abode to find that his wife had got fed up with the two large animals and sold them.

Thereafter, in the yard, he was called Dugless!

+   +   +

'Did ye know that Helen o' Troy's face launched a thoosan' ships?'

'Must have knocked her pan in hittin' aw they hulls.'

+   +   +

A traditional story goes that one of the shipyard owners on the Clyde was recognised by the King for his services to industry, and was duly summoned to Buckingham Palace to receive his knighthood. The owner thought it would be a nice gesture if, along with his wife, he were to take one of the senior shop stewards from his yard, just to show everyone what a caring employer he was.

At the ceremony in the Palace, it came the turn of the shipyard owner to kneel before His Majesty. However when the

King said, 'Arise, Sir ********', the Clyde industrialist didn't move. Again the king said, in a slightly louder tone, 'ARISE, SIR ********.' Again there was no movement.

Just then the wee shop steward shouted out. 'Ye'd better jist tell him tae get up, yer Majesty. He disnae know whit a rise is!'

+   +   +

A more modern shipyard tale:

The reinforced glass for windows on a ship being built on the Clyde were being supplied by a Spanish company. However the glass delivery was well behind schedule. So, it was agreed with the Spaniards that the window frames should be fitted to the vessel, and the Spanish company send two of their men over when the glass became available, and they would fit the panes.

As it happened, only one man arrived and he had no English. However, he sang to himself in Spanish as he worked. It wasn't long before the Clyde's propensity of conferring nicknames on workers was fulfilled. He became known as 'Hulio the Glazier'. (Julio Iglesias!)

+   +   +

A bow-legged woman, employed as a sweeper-upper in the yard, was one day frightened by a rat. 'Jump on the bleedin' thing!' shouted some workers nearby. So she bravely jumped but the rat ran through her legs and escaped. She turned round to the workers and explained, 'Sorry, but ma legs is only built fur goin' roon corners.'

+   +   +

Sandy was a keen apprentice working under the eagle eye of an experienced journeyman joiner. Towards the end of a day the foreman approached, and asked Sandy how he had got on that day. 'Och, jist fine,' replied Sandy. 'ah cut oot twinty jigs the day.'

'That's grand,' replied the foreman, to which the over-enthusiastic Sandy replied. 'It wis really thirty, but ah wis telt tae keep the ither yins up ma sleeve fur the morra.'

The journeyman looked at the foreman with a weak smile. 'Ah cannae believe this. Up 'big-mouth's' sleeve? Ah'll stick them up his erse!'

+ + +

It was the Glasgow half-marathon. One of the entrants had filled in his application form as being 98. This was giving some concern to the race officials.

'Do you think you will be able to run the distance?' he was asked by the race medical team.

'Run the distance! Listen, if ye gae me a three yard start ah'll win it.'

'Just three yards?'

'Aye, Stephens, Fairfields and John Browns!'

+ + +

The old plater made his way slowly across the cobbles of the yard. It was raining and his shabby clothes were soaked through. As he walked a flapping sound could be heard. The sole of a boot had come off and was slapping against the cobbles.

A tall, dignified man holding an umbrella was also making his way across the yard; the shipyard owner. Seeing his worker's predicament he shouted. 'Come here, man. We can't have you walking about like that.' Taking a wad of notes from his inside pocket he removed the elastic band around them. 'Here,' he said 'put that round your boot.'

One of the ladies from the tracing office was retiring. A wee presentation of flowers was planned. The young office manager made a short speech thanking Mrs Miller for her long and sterling work. In reply she said, 'Thanks fur the flooers. Jist tae correct ye. Ah'm no' a Mrs, ah'm a Miss. But it's ok, son, ah'll no' die wonderin'!'

+   +   +

'Here's a question fur ye, Shug,' posed the foreman. 'If a train stoaps at the Central Station, an' ah bus stoaps at Buchanan Street Station, whit stoaps at a work station?'

'Ah, don't know,' answered Wee Shug.

'The answer's you! Noo, get a bleedin' move oan.'

+   +   +

'Hey, Gerry!' exclaimed the foreman. 'Dae you believe in life efter death?'

'Aye,' replied Gerry, 'ah dae.'

'Well, ah'm awfa pleased,' said his foreman. 'Yesterday, jist efter the lunch break, when you left tae go tae yer friend Billy's funeral, he came intae the yard looking fur a start!'

+   +   +

The new apprentice was told to sweep up steel cuttings from the floor. 'Hey,' he protested to his journeyman, 'ah'm here tae learn. Ah've goat ma highers?'

'Sorry,' replied the journeyman, 'they didnae tell me that. Here, gie's that brush an' ah'll show ye hoo tae dae it!'.

+   +   +

'Swan Lake' was a rivet boy up until redundancy at the age of 60. Despite working in the harsh environment of the yards all his life, 'Swan Lake' had sophisticated tastes, was well read, and had a great passion for ballet, hence his nickname.

As a single man he was able to travel to various ballets

throughout Europe.

.The year after he was made redundant, 'Swan Lake' was in London at Covent Garden. As was his way, he arrived early for the performance. He sat in the stalls reading through the programme, eagerly anticipating the coming performance, savouring his surroundings. Around him the theatre was gradually filling up.

'Swan Lake' became conscious that immediately behind him a young man and two young ladies had sat down. Then he heard loud, boastful tones obviously coming from the ladies' male escort. The young females were swooning over their escort. He could hear them say, 'Yes, Nigel.' 'Oh, how divine, Nigel'. Suddenly, 'Swan Lake' became aware that the back of his seat was rocking back and forth; the young man had put his feet up on its back.

Politely, 'Swan Lake' turned around and quietly said, 'Excuse me, Nigel. I wonder if I could kindly ask you not to put your feet on the back of my seat. Thank you so much.'

When 'Swan Lake' resumed his forward position, he heard the young man immediately snort and say, 'Did you hear that Scottish person calling me Nigel? Such familiarity, and we haven't even been introduced!' The back of 'Swan Lake's' seat was then kicked, and it rocked back and forth even more vigorously as all three people behind laughed and giggled.

'Swan Lake' sighed, closed his programme, and slowly stood up to his full five feet two inches. Then he turned round, took a deep breath, and yelled at the top of his voice, 'Get yer bloody feet aff the back o' ma seat or ah'll belt yer coupon fae here tae kingdom come!'

Nigel and his companions sat ashen faced. Silence immediately fell over the auditorium. Swan Lake quietly resumed his seat and again consulted his programme.

During the entire ballet no sound or movement came from behind. 'Swan Lake' sat, lost in the rich tapestry of the performance.

Aye, ye can take the man oot the yairds, but ye cannae take the yairds oot the man!

+   +   +

A red-leader was assigned the task by his foreman, of _ _ _ leading the top of a tall crane.

Looking up at the crane, the man commented. 'Hey, ah'm a red-leader, no' a squadron leader!'

+   +   +

Two ladies at a bus stop got to chatting. 'Whit does your man dae?' asked one wee woman.

'Oh,' said the superior-looking one, 'He has a very responsible position in the shipyards. I'll have you know he's a holder-on. And what does your husband do.'

'Och, he's jist a hauder-oan!'

+   +   +

'So why were ye no' at yer work yesterday?' demanded the foreman, 'Wee Fred the Red'.

'Ma fether-in-law goat burnt,' came the reply.

'Wis he badly burnt?'

'Listen, they don't muck aboot up at the cremmy.'

+   +   +

In many shipyard families it was traditional for the wife to handle the money, hence the expression. 'Aye, he's a guid man. Disnae gie her a broken pey.' Or if the wife was a domineering sort, it was said, 'Ah widnae like tae tak a broken pey hame tae her!' (A broken pey being one where the envelope containing the wage money had been opened by the husband and some of its contents removed (usually for drink), prior to handing it over to his wife.) It was not unknown for the wife to open the 'pay-poke' and give her husband some coins with the warning, 'There's yer money. An' remember noo, it's jist fur the jinglin'!'

+   +   +

Some wives would stand across the road from the yard gates on pay-night, usually resplendent in headscarfs, with a hint of metal curlers beneath, wearing slippers and apron.

As one worker observed, when he saw the line of wives waiting on their man's pay-poke before he got to the pub, 'If Thistle had a half-back line like that they widnae need a goalie!'

+   +   +

6

Shipyard patter

At the end of the lunch-break the chargehand walked passed three workers, still sitting in the sunshine, backs to a wall.

    'Right, that's the horn gone,' he observed sharply.

    'Aye,' came a voice, 'ye cannae trust anybuddy in this yard. But it wisnae us!'

+   +   +

'When it comes tae work there's many in this yard will stop at nothing.'

+   +   +

'Hey, you up there!' shouted 'Dreepie Wullie', the foreman. 'Nae singing fitba' songs while yer workin'!'

    'Who's workin'?

+   +   +

'Ah'm thinkin' o' becomin' a vegetarian,' said Wee Fergus.

    'Aye, then ye can pap peas at baith yer granny and the gaffer!'

+   +   +

'So, yer a smart wee fella, Jimmy, ur ye?' asked his journeyman. 'Right, ah'll gae ye a shipping test. Whit dae ye get if you
cross the Atlantic wi' the *Titanic*?'
    'Ah don't know, Bill.'
    'Half-way, ya dope!'

+   +   +

'Aw, naw. The foreman's comin'!'
    'Aye, it's 'Big Sid'. Says mair then his prayers he does …
an' he whistles them!'

+   +   +

'Whit dae ye take me fur?' exclaimed the rivet-boy. 'Ah've only
goat two pairs o' hauns, ye know!'

+   +   +

'Huv ye ever given up the bevvy, Sammy?'
    'Aye, wance oan the night shift. It wis the worst ten hours
o' ma life!'

+   +   +

'Mean bastard, that gaffer. Widnae gie ye a fright oan a dark
night.'
    'Aye, we're lucky he's no' wan o' twins.'

+   +   +

'Freezin up here, intit?' commented Kenny, a member of the
local pipe band.
    'Aye. Ye'll be glad yer no' a 'kiltie kiltie cauld bum' the day.'

+   +   +

'Whit's the difference between a plater an' a riveter, mister?'
    'Aboot threepence an hour.'

+   +   +

'Dae ye no' think that workin' in the yards is like livin' in the Dark Ages?'

'Aye, an' if they close this place we'll aw be history.'

+   +   +

'Come here you,' said the foreman, beckoning over 'Willie-the-Slouch'. 'Let me tell you, you've hardly done a hand's turn the day. Dae ye no' know that hard work never killed anybuddy?'

'Well, ye see, ah didnae want tae take a chance!'

+   +   +

'Dae ye think they'll ever write a book aboot this new liner we're building, Pat?'

'Aye, an' if you don't get they plates oan right they'll call it *Twenty Thoosand Leagues Under the Sea!*

+   +   +

'Ma big brither that left the yard last year is noo a man o' letters.'

'Ah didnae know he wis a postie!'

+   +   +

Fumes in a hold had overcome Erchie. As he was being carried into the ambulance, the ambulance man asked, 'Gie's yer name so we can tell yer family.'

'But ma family already know ma name,' came the reply.

+   +   +

'Get oan wi' yer work and get those hands oot yer pockets,' the chargehand shouted at 'See you, Jimmy'.

'Ah cannae. Ma braces are broke!'

+   +   +

'Dae ye know whit ah wid like tae dae tae that big blond stoater up in the offices?' exclaimed the apprentice to the journeyman.

'Naw. An' jist whit would you like tae dae tae ma daughter?' came the reply.

'Oh! Is yon yer daughter? Lovely big lassie that!'

+   +   +

The two boilermakers were having a break. 'You at that bottle again, 'Wee Man'. Ah wis jist readin' in the *Sunday Post* that alcohol is really a slow poison.'

'That's aw right. Ah'm no' in a hurry!'

+   +   +

'Ah'm no' masel' the day,' said the plater. 'Jist cannae get goin'.'

'Aye, ah could tell that tae look at ye. Ye look like the first husband o' a wee widow wummin!

+   +   +

'Whit's a gizinty?' 'See you, Jimmy' asked his journeyman.

'Hey, see that bolt that won't go intae that plate? Well, pass me that sledgehammer an' ah'll show ye whit a gizinty is.'

+   +   +

'See yon gaffer. Talks through the wee hole in his erse.'

'Aye, he's aye bummin' his chat.'

+   +   +

'Ah'm chokinfurra pee.

'Well if that's the case it's no' a lavvy ye need, it's a plumber!'

+   +   +

'Well at least the boys on the night shift are no' afraid of hard work. They can go to sleep right beside it.'

+   +   +

'When you're oot oan trials wi' a ship are ye ever seasick?

　'Seasick! Listen, the first thing ah dae is fling ma pieces o'er the side. It saves me time!'

+   +   +

In the confined space of a small cabin Wee Murray let off a stinker. 'Where'er ye be, let yer wind gae free,' he immediately quoted.

　'Listen, Murray,' said his mate, 'a left-handed burner could dae a couple o' plates wi' the gas you've jist let off!'

+   +   +

It was lunchbreak and the squad were sitting in their wee howf. 'Whit ye daein', Wullie?'

　'Ah'm jist working oot the family allowance ah'm gonna get fur the new wean we're havin'. Jings, ah reckon ah'm gonna get £45 pounds this year.'

　'Don't be daft, man, ye'll never get that much. Ye only get it fae when it comes oot, naw when it went in!'

+   +   +

'Whit kind o' steel-tipped boots dae they supply ye wi' in this yard?'

　'Two kinds. Too big or too small!'

+   +   +

'Pit yer back intae it. Ah think you're jist pretending tae work.'

　'Yer right. The management here pretend tae pay me, so ah pretend tae work!'

+   +   +

'Ah see the union has goat us two nights an' a half-day Sunday overtime.'

'Aye, well at least it's better than a skelp in the face wi' a Loch Fyne haddie's uncle.'

+ + +

When the *QE2* was having fitting-out work carried out downriver, one of the managers paid a visit to a local, less than fashionable housing estate. When asked why he had done this, he replied. 'Sentimental reasons. Ah jist like tae keep in touch wi' aw ma cabin furniture!'

+ + +

'Oh, my, Mrs MacDougall,' said her next door neighbour. 'Whit a lovely, big, thick new tartan carpet. Yer man must be workin' oan the new Queen!'

+ + +

'Yon's thick! Listen if we wis oot oan trials in a submarine he wid open the windae tae get some fresh air!

+ + +

'Ur they two boats diesel?'
  'Aye.'
  'Will they sail far?'
  'Diesel sail roon the world!'

+ + +

'Whit time dae ye start tae work?'
  'Och, aboot an hour efter ah clock on!'

+ + +

'Where's the best place fur a haircut?'

'Wee Sammy wull gie ye a haircut up in the blacksmith's shop.'

'Is he ony good?'

'Useless. But his patter's great. He's the only wan that knows whit's goin' on in this yard.'

+   +   +

'See that wee lassie up in the offices wi' the white face. Looks like a tart at a dance.'

'Mair like a fart in a trance!'

+   +   +

'Whit aboot the bonus oan this joab.'

'Och, the gaffer will share it oot eexy, peexy.'

'Whit does that mean?'

'Wan tae you and two tae him.'

+   +   +

'This rivet won't fit in the bleedin' hole.'

'Keep at it, son. Remember, if at first ye don't succeed, hit it wi' a lump o' breed, If again ye don't succeed, then in wi' the boot an' wan wi' the heid!'

+   +   +

'Watch out fur that right beezer o' a foreman, he does bird impressions. Wid have ye 'quartered' as soon as look at ye.'

'Ye mean he whistles like a nightingale?'

'Naw! Ah mean he watches ye like a hawk!'

+   +   +

'Ye've goat a face on ye like a welder's bench.'

'Och away an' wipe yer bahookie wi' a toffee apple.'

+   +   +

'Whit's the matter? Been at the bevvy? Yer nose looks like a plook on a half-skelped arse.'

+   +   +

'How lang have you been workin' here?'

'Jist since the foreman went his dinger an' threatened tae bag me!'

+   +   +

'Yon's a big balloon, that charge-hand. Full o' gas. Wan good fart an' he'd be headin' doon the Clyde tae Rothesay.'

+   +   +

'Is yon wee tracer thin? She'd need tae stand twice in the wan spot tae make a shadow.'

+   +   +

'Ah hear Smithie went tae gie blood at the mobile transfusion van outside the yard.'

'How did he get oan?'

'They told him that if they ever needed pints o' heavy they would send him a letter!'

+   +   +

'Is there much mair work left oan this boat?'

'Don't you worry, pal. You've a lot mair damage tae dae afore this boat is finished.'

+   +   +

'That big chanty-wrastler o' a charge-hand jist opens his big mooth an' lets his belly rumble.'

'Watch whit ye say aboot him, especially as you've nae teeth. Remember, 'dinnae tie a knot in yer tongue ye cannae undo wi' yer teeth!''

+   +   +

'That bampot o' a wee wuman painter is as auld as her tongue and a gey bit older than her teeth.'

+   +   +

'If yer corrie-fistit then ye'll get a start. They're aye looking fur left-handed riveters.'

+   +   +

Notice outside a Clyde Shipyard.
'Today's launch has been called off due to flooding.'

+   +   +

'Look at aw they chookiebirdies circlin' up there,' observed the plater pointing to the circulating seagulls. 'Is nature no' great?'

'Aye, but wan o' yer chookiebirdies has just shat on yer cadie.'

+   +   +

'Right, ah'm awa' tae see a friend aff tae sea.'
'Is wan o' yer pals going away oan a boat?' asked the apprentice.
'Don't be daft, son. I'm away tae the shitterooterie!'
'The shitterooterie?'
'Aye, have ye never heard o' the expression, 'Yer bum's oot the windae? Well in oor shitterooterie it sticks through the flair!'

+   +   +

Two shipyard workers were having a final refreshment in a Glasgow pub. 'Ah've been in the yards since ah wis ah lad. Shipbuilding is in ma soul. Ah've even goat a boat-hoose, an' noo ah've been paid aff.'

'Ah didnae know ye had a boat-hoose.'

'Aye, sure ah boat it fae the Corporation.'

+   +   +

'Fur heaven's sake don't get that daft lout o' an apprentice tae dae that wee job. Yon's daft. He'd stick his heid through a porthole an' go outside tae shove it back in again'!'

+   +   +

'The management in this yard couldnae run a four-door cludgie painted tartan at the hoors' annual ball!'

+   +   +

The apprentice said to the journeyman, 'Gie's o'er a match.'

The journeyman gave him a smack on the ear with the observation, 'Here you. Yer heid's waistit! Huv youse never heard o' the word goannae?'

+   +   +

'See that foreman's wife. She's a right wee snob noo she lives up a half-tiled wally close.'

'Och, ah remember her when she ran aboot wi' nae knickers. A real honey fae the dunny. Noo ah bet she wears they 'passion-killers''.

Note: 'Passion-killers' were large pink Celanese knickers with elastic around the knee.

+   +   +

The men's toilet was a mess. Urine had overflowed all over the floor. The stench was unbearable.

Those inside held their breath while quickly trying to relieve themselves and escape the smell. Suddenly a knocking was heard on the outside door of the urinal. One of the occupants shouted.

'Come on in, if yer feet's clean!'

+　　　+　　　+

'Dae ye fancy that big stoater that's in the tracing department?'

'Her! Listen, ah widna go oot wi' her if she farted two bob bits at the weekend and tanners the rest o' the week!'

+　　　+　　　+

'Whit ye drinkin, big man, alang wi' yer piece?'

'Sugaralliewatter, but it's mines.'

'Stoapyergirnin an' geezasook o' yer bottle!'

+　　　+　　　+

'Who are ye workin' fur this weather?'

'Och, the same lot,' the riveter replied. 'The wife, ma dug and five weans.'

+　　　+　　　+

The apprentice had queued up at the counter of the yard store. When it came his turn he casually observed to the storeman. 'Ye know, it's been more than eighteen months since ah first came here.'

'Well, ah can only serve wan at a time,' replied the harassed storeman.

+　　　+　　　+

'Ye cannae be up tae you,' observed the charge hand. 'You've made a right erse o' that joab, haven't ye?'

'Well, we were a bit behind!'

+   +   +

'See that charge-hand, he'd pee the bed an' blame the blankets.'

+   +   +

'Look at that wee French polisher o'er there. Ah bet she's a right sexy bit o' stuff.'

'Her, sexy! Yon widnae hing oot her knickers oan the line in case it gave the man next door a thrill.'

+   +   +

'Dae ye think the edge on this plate is alright? It looks gie rough tae me.'

'Listen, a blind man runnin' fur a tram tae Partick oan a dark night widna even notice!'

+   +   +

'So whit wull drive this boat when we've goat her finished?' asked the wee apprentice.

'Turbines, son.'

'Ah thought turbines wis whit Injuns wore oan their heids.'

+   +   +

'See this riveting game. Sure it's jist like being a dentist daein fillings.'

'Aye, but he disnae huv tae haud up a rivet gun aw day. Anyway, wi' aw this shakin' aboot ah'm gonnae huv tae get a set o' new wallies.'

+   +   +

'Jings your wife has made ye up a rare lunch the day. Is that a macaroon ah see or a meringue?'

'Naw, yer right! It's a macaroon!'

'Ye know, the Clyde runs through ma veins.'

'Aye, plus electric soup, pints o' heavy an' a few haufs!'

+ + +

'Ah fine like the joab, mister. It's jist the work ah hate.'

+ + +

The timekeeper was in a belligerent mood, and he shouted at 'Wee Brian'.

'See you! Yer the only man in this yard that gets tae work late and makes up fur it by trying tae leave early!'

+ + +

'Has the horn no' gone yet? Ah'm famished. Ah could eat a scabbie dug.'

'Never seen wan. But ah've often seen a green dug.'

+   +   +

'Ah used tae be a white collar worker up in the offices.'

'So whit happened yer noo' doon in the yard?'

'Ma collar goat dirty.'

+   +   +

'Last week ah goat a bare pey.'

'Jist be thankful. If ye didnae get a pey ye'd be runnin' aboot wi' a bare erse!'

+   +   +

Porky-the-Plater's grace each day before he ate his sandwiches.
'Three slices fur the wan o' us,
Thank guidness there's nae mair o' us,
Happy and Glorious,
God save the King.'

+   +   +

'That skitterie wee labourer does nothing but sook in wi' the gaffer.'

'Yer right. Wid let him slug a scoosh o' his last pint, yon wan.'

+   +   +

'Bet ye've never worked a day in yer life in this yard.'
    'Yer right. Ah've aye been oan constant nightshift.'

+   +   +

'When ah tell ye him in the blacksmith's shop wis legless on
Saturday night, whit ah mean is, he could lie oan the flair
withoot haudin' on!'

+   +   +

There was a horse in the yard used to pull a cart, mostly
delivering rivets or collecting scrap. One of the apprentices
painted on the back of the cart in large white letters, 'Do not
step on the exhaust fumes!'

7

Shipyard 'cairry-oans'!

In some yards the toilets consisted of running water flowing along an open culvert, through somewhat squalid toilet cubicles. Workers had to crouch over this flow. Sometimes the occupant of the end stall would set a newspaper on fire before floating it down the stream of water, causing much anguish among the straining workers!

+   +   +

The painters in the yards were mostly women; a determined lot who stopped for nobody. One day a squad entered a cabin where workmen had left their toolboxes. When the men returned they found every box painted white, and when they moved them, the deck under the toolboxes remained unpainted.

The following day, the same squad of women started

painting a cable at the same time as men on
deck were hauling it onboard. The workmen
suddenly found themselves pulling on cable
dripping with paint. One cheeky apprentice
shouted down at the women, complaining
bitterly with a few ill-chosen words. Minutes
later the 'ladies' appeared on deck, pouncing
on their abuser and pinning him to the deck.
Down came the dungarees, and his 'privates'
were all painted white, while disparaging
remarks were made as to its size.

   One of those wild girls was later to become
his wife. 'Ah've seen it aw before,' she
commented to a knowing friend at the wedding.
'Ah jist hope he's washed the paint aff!'

✚   ✚   ✚

Many apprentices ran the savage gauntlet of nubile yard
women, who reacted to cheeky blood-racing, teasing comments.
Some apprentices ended up naked, their clothes floating in the
Clyde.

✚   ✚   ✚

When one of the girls in the yard was leaving or getting married,
it was common for her to be dressed up in net curtains,
decorated with the likes of rhubarb and cauliflower, a dummy
put in her mouth, before being paraded around the yard. Then,
for luck, she had to jump over an enamel potty filled with 'the
salt of life', wee dolls and sweets. Many of these potties were
specially bought because they had a message printed around the
side: 'Wash me well and keep me clean, and I won't tell what I
have seen'. Then the girl in question might be put on the back
of a lorry and taken home in all her finery!

   This ceremony was referred to as a 'booking'.

✚   ✚   ✚

In the drawing office a bridegroom-to-be would be dressed up by the tracers. But beforehand, it was commonplace for him to be carried shoulder-high to 'the bog' by his fellows and there be imprinted with a selection of stamps normally applied to drawings. Many's the unfortunate on his wedding night who still bore, on a very personal part of his anatomy, an indelible message such as 'Not to be used without instruction'!

+   +   +

'See you, Jimmy' was assigned to work with a journeyman who, although a skilled worker, was limited in his speech process. This was exemplified by the time he told the lad to go to the store and get him a 'wee hingmybob'.

+   +   +

'Tone–the-Moan', never a happy worker, found a great way of 'half-inching' copper welding cable out the yard gates. Ten minutes before the finishing horn, he would adjourn to the urinals where he would strip and wind the cable around his body, emerging somewhat fatter.

The scam went on for weeks without mishap, until the day 'Tone-the-Moan' came running out the gates in the middle of the usual exodus, only to trip and fall. Although unhurt, he found himself unable to get up due to his new found bulk and weight. He lay upside down, with his arms and legs moving, for all the world like an upturned tortoise.

One of the yard commissionaires came over to help him to his feet. The guard tried to pull him up, then surmised the problem. Needless to say, 'Tone-the-Moan' then had something to moan about.

+   +   +

Big Donald's squad were fond of their pints, none more so than Big Donald himself. When there was no money around Big Donald would convince the foreman that one of the squad had to be paid off immediately. When he got the money the squad would then adjourn to the nearby pub. They would however leave their plates being heated while they were there, so no time was lost.

The following day Big Donald would convince the foreman that he couldn't get on without this man who, as it just happened, was at that very moment at the yard gates!

The gaffer knew what the ploy was, but as they were one of the hardest working squads in the yard, he reckoned they were worth keeping.

+ + +

Rab was an under-gaffer in a boilermakers' shop. A tall man with an arrogant air on his finely chiselled face, set off by sharp, black eyes – someone with a vile temper, a man not to be crossed.

Big Rab was also a man of habit. Always half-an-hour early at work in the morning, he left the yard quarter of an hour after his squad at night. At the midday break he always went through the same routine. First of all he sat by himself eating sandwiches and drinking from his flask. Next he squatted behind a huge piles of metal plates for his daily 'number two.' (It saved him a long walk to the men's toilets.) His habits were, of course, well known to the squad.

One day as he squatted behind the piles of metal, a shovel with a very long handle, specially made by the men, was quietly slipped beneath his posterior. When he had finished, he duly pulled up his long-johns, his trousers and then his overalls, before looking behind him to see the result of his efforts. Nothing was there! As his mind had been elsewhere during his efforts, he again removed his overalls, his trousers and long-johns and went through the whole process again to no avail. Just then he heard laughter. Looking up he saw the squad in front of him, holding the loaded shovel. 'Is this whit yer lookin' fur, Rab?'

Big Rab laughed ... eventually.

+ + +

Bobbie was a wee rascal, someone with a reckless determination about him who should have been given his 'books' on many an occasion. Workers would find themselves stuck to the deck as Bobbie gave their steel-capped boots a zap with his welder's torch.

One day he got a brown paper poke, blew it up with flammable gas from his oxyacetylene torch, before tying the neck. Passing the rivet-boy's fire he tossed it in. The resulting explosion blew charcoal over a wide area and nearly injured a couple of the men.

+ + +

It was 'See you, Jimmy's' second day in the yard. One of the men asked him to go to the store, and get him a bubble for his spirit level as he wanted to make sure that the ship was on an even keel! And while he was at it could he get a 'sky-hook', just in case the ship was not lying true and had to be lifted. If he couldn't get them in the store then he'd find them in the stowaway's locker!

+ + +

Another time 'See you, Jimmy' was sent to the Engineering Shop for a set of testicles. 'Sorry, son,' said the storeman, 'but mine's are too big fur ye.'

+ + +

Pranks were continually being played on new apprentices. 'See you, Jimmy' was asked by one of the men to get a bucket of blue steam. Some half-an-hour later 'See you, Jimmy' returned to tell the man that they only had white steam in the store, and as it was costly, he would need to come and sign for it himself!

+ + +

New apprentices got suspicious after a while when asked to run errands. Especially if they were asked to nip round to the stores and get tins of compression, keys for the keel, tartan paint or left-handed screwdrivers.

+   +   +

In some yards, on the last working day of the year, everyone who arrived in the office areas after the official starting time, was 'banged in'. Everyone, be they draughtsmen, tracers or admin staff, would thump their fists on boards and tables from the moment the unfortunate latecomer opened the door until he or she reached their workstation.

This tradition was called 'skitterie winter', originally the last person to leave work on Hogmanay.

+   +   +

'Is a plater mair important than an engineer?' 'See you, Jimmy' asked a journeyman.

'He certainly is, son. Engineers have tae work tae tens o' thousands o' an inch, but us platers huv tae get it right!'

+   +   +

The foreman asked the apprentice, 'How many thousands are there in an inch?'

'Och, there must be millions o' the wee buggers!'

+   +   +

The yard manager was approached by one of the cost estimators, who asked, 'Mister McLelland, dae ye think we could build a trawler in this yard?'

'Listen, son,' replied the yard manager, 'a plater and his dug could build half-a-dozen trawlers in this yard.'

'Why a dug, Mister McLelland?'

'Tae tell the plater whit tae dae, son!'

+   +   +

Yard management were showing some government officials around, impressing them with the efficiency of the place and clearly hoping for future orders. As the party crossed the yard, a plate being hoisted was caught in a gust of wind, slipping off its sling and crashing to the ground. 'Fire the man responsible!' shouted the managing director.

The yard manager went over to the slinger, and recognised him as one of the best workers in the yard. 'You're fired!' he yelled. 'Collect your books at the gate right noo!' Then in a whisper added, 'An' start again the morn!'

+ + +

The ship was getting behind schedule. The specification for the portholes was for one-inch thick glass. The supplier had none and it would be weeks before it became available. So 'fix-it Fred' was consulted, one of the gaffers who always had a solution to any problem.

When the ship sailed, all the portholes consisted of two half-inch glass plates stuck together.

+ + +

Singing and hysterical laughter could be heard coming from a paint squad (of men), deep in the bilges. Repeated shouts by their gaffer for the squad to stop their nonsense and come on deck were ignored. The problem went on for a couple of hours and eventually the yard manager phoned the police. A squad car arrived with two constables. They slowly made their way down to the painters. The policemen however failed to reappear. By this time a further police car had appeared, and its occupants also went below to find out what had happened to their colleagues. They, too, did not reappear. Indeed the singing and laughter if anything was getting louder.

The fire brigade came, and wearing breathing apparatus they made their way below. Ten minutes later they reappeared with the painters and policemen, still all singing and giggling.

In transpired that the extractor fans in the bowels of the ship had fused and the paint fumes had overcome the revellers!

+ + +

The men's toilets in the office area of a certain shipyard were really not too bad. Certainly much better than in the yard.

One day one of the senior yard managers entered the office toilet. As he was washing his hands, he heard a repetitive clicking noise coming from one of the cubicles. Looking beneath the cubicle door, he was confused and indeed worried to see two pairs of feet, one set pointing out, the other set pointing inwards.

Just then one of the office-boys entered the toilet and, immediately sizing up the situation, shouted, 'Hey, Freddie. Ur ye gonnae be lang? Wan o' the managers is waiting fur a wee trim.'

To which came the response, 'Ah'll no' be a minute. An' tell him I'll dae his hair fur nothin' this time!'

+   +   +

Working in the confined space of a ship's double-bottom was both demanding and restricting. Having struggled through small openings and tiny compartment doors, it was impractical to come all the way back, along with tools and equipment, to go to the toilet. Therefore it was generally accepted that an individual could carry out his bodily functions within the ship's double-bottom. In one particular yard, Alex, an old bevvy merchant, was paid extra money to go in and remove the 'jobbies'. He was paid on a piecework basis, until it was discovered that in some instances he halved the offending 'jobbie' and claimed two!

+   +   +

One of the men told his chargehand he would need to get off on Wednesday in three weeks' time, as he had to attend a funeral. The chargehand thought this somewhat unusual, but reckoned that the person concerned was perhaps in the final stages of dying. A week later the man approached his charge hand, with the reassuring news that he would no longer require time off for the funeral as it was cancelled, 'They didnae get through tae the next round!' he explained.

+   +   +

Times were tough! The sub-contractors all lined up of a Friday to get their wages. A line formed in front of their manager as he shouted out a name and gave each man a pay-poke. As one of the men reached out for his money, the manager punched his employee on the jaw, knocking him flying.

'Hey. Whit did ye dae that fur?' said the assaulted man.

'That's fur no' comin' in oan time oan Wednesday!'

+   +   +

A director of a certain yard went by the name of Innisfree. He openly boasted that all his household requirements came from the yard; the painting of his home, the maintenance of the grounds, even light bulbs all originated in the shipyard.

He was known by the men as 'Itsawfree'!

+   +   +

With the abuse of yard manpower and purchasing by the bosses, 'homers' by the workers became common. Everything from trolleys for golf clubs, girds for children, to garden rollers were produced.

+   +   +

By now 'See You, Jimmy' was continually on his guard against the pranks that were played on the young lads in the shipyard. So when he was asked to go across the road and get vegetables and fruit for the donkey diesel engines, he was able to give the standard reply,

'DaeyethinkahcomeuptheClydeoanabanannaboat!'

A further request to go and collect a tin of 'elbow grease' was given the same contemptuous remark.

+   +   +

One of the wags in the yard caught a couple of pigeons and stuck them in a locker. When the owner of the locker opened it, the terrified birds flew passed him like bats out of hell. As the worker commented later, after he had calmed down, 'It wis enough tae drive ye 'doo-lally'!

+   +   +

One day 'Wee Malky' appeared with a tailor's dummy. He then proceeded to dress it in an old pair of overalls and bunnet, and leave it against a workbench. When the gaffer came round he took a minute or two before realising the figure was just a dummy. He commented, 'As lang as ye don't think he's getting a pey oan Friday.'

The dummy stayed in its position for a number of weeks. Then one morning Wee Malky took the clothes off the dummy, hid it under the bench and put the same overall and bunnet on himself. He stationed himself in exactly the same way as the dummy had stood. When the foreman did his rounds the dummy suddenly 'came to life', shouting, 'where's ma pey?'

The foreman stood back, shocked, before saying. 'It's up wi' the timekeeper. Yer fired, ya dummy!'

+   +   +

Peter-the-overtaker was an enthusiastic cyclist, and had got his name because he was well known for zig-zagging through traffic at high speed. Every night he could be found behind the huge yard gates, mingling with those men who had a physical handicap, waiting for the gates to open so he could speed off home ahead of the mad dash. Outside the gate a policeman held up traffic until the mass charge got out the yard at the end of their day.

One day the policeman failed to turn up on time and the gateman decided to open the gate with traffic still flowing outside. Peter screamed off on his bike in his usual manner, only to find himself directly behind a slow moving hearse and in front of a line of taxis containing the principal mourners, all going to a local church. Not wishing to be disrespectful and overtake a hearse, he slowly cycled behind the hearse until it got to the church some miles away. After this incident his name in the yard was changed to Peter-the-Undertaker!

+   +   +

John arrived home late one Friday night. It was immediately obvious that he had imbibed of a 'wee refreshment or four'. 'Right!' demanded his somewhat overbearing wife, 'wher's the pay-poke.'

'Well, ye see, ma darlin'', replied John, ' ah hud a wee bit o' bother on the way hame fae the yard. Ma pey poke fell oan the street, an' a wee dug ate it. Ah've only goat two pounds and two shillings left tae gie ye.'

His wife grabbed the two pounds. 'Right, you,' she rasped, 'keep the two bob and away an' buy the dug!'

+   +   +

The yard owner came into the machine shop. 'You'll be replacing all these leather belts on your machines soon?' he enquired of the gaffer.

'Aye, sur, next week in fact,' came the reply.

'Good. Well, waste not, want not. Sole these.' Taking out a bag he flung his family's shoes on the floor.

+   +   +

The three carpet fitters made a lovely job of laying a top-of-the-range carpet, wall to wall, in one of the state rooms of the new liner. The following morning all that remained of the carpet was a six-inch strip around the wall.

'Whit's happen? Where's oor carpet?' wailed one of the carpet layers.

'It's at the Barras!'

It's 18 yds short, this carpet you've sent us –

One of the men gave an apprentice a wee pup he had found wandering in the yard. The lad took it home, put it in a cardboard box of straw and fed it. However it just lay there unmoving. So the lad took it to the local Cat and Dog Home to get advice.

'Advice, son,' said the man, 'Ah'll tell ye whit tae dae. Pit that rat back in the sewer ye found it in!'

✛   ✛   ✛

The Royal 'We'.

It was announced that one of the Royal princesses was coming to launch a vessel. This immediately gave the 'high-heid-yins' a problem; there wasn't a suitable ladies toilet in the yard.

A portaloo was procured. It was cleaned, sanitised and painted in preparation for the great day. No one was allowed to use the facility, and the key to its door safely retained in the inside pocket of a trusty foreman.

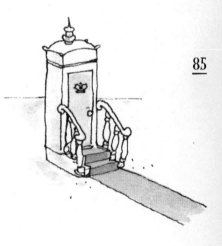

The great day came and the Princess and her ladies-in-waiting duly arrived. After the initial welcome, they opted to 'wash their hands'. When the Royal person entered the portaloo, she found a large jobby bobbing in the wc and a sign on the wall which read, 'Kilroy wis here!'

✛   ✛   ✛

Sure enough, 'See you, Jimmy' fell victim to the oldest prank in the yard. He dutifully went to the stores to find a 'long weight'. It was only after being told to stand in the corner for five minutes that it suddenly dawned on him!

✛   ✛   ✛

85

A fleet of buses awaited the men at the yard gates each night. On one particular route going to an area of Glasgow, it was always the same conductress, a young, vivacious girl who enjoyed swapping banter with the men. Over the weeks the workers started to slip her their fares saying, 'Dinnae gie us a ticket. Jist you keep it fur yersel, hen'

A few weeks later when they came out of the yard they found that their bus had been taken off the route. The shop steward was informed, and he in turn spoke to the bus company. It had been stopped as no one appeared to be using the service!

8

'See you Jimmy!' remembers

It was standing on the deck of the *QE2* looking at the ocean that brought back the memories. Aye, sure enough, he could still remember his first day in the yard as though it was yesterday.

As he had come over the hill he had seen the waves on the water. They were as the hue of slate but with occasional brown ripples interspersed with 'white horses'. The banks of the Clyde grew narrow at that point, with the water thrusting against the far shoreline.

Gusts had torn at his new bunnet and flapped at the legs of his dungarees. An assortment of huge cranes prodded at the sky, rearing over the housetops like cows looking over a dyke. A profusion of tenement roofs stretched into the horizon. Seagulls shrieked and cried above. As he neared the yard he could hear the sound of men's voices, the beat of boots, see the spirals of cigarette smoke dissipating above their heads. He was nervous, very nervous.

All his life he could remember seeing the vigil of clusters of men standing outside the yard gates waiting for a 'start'.

Regardless of whether it was rain, sleet or snow, there they were, shabbily dressed men in cloth bunnets, thin scarves and dungarees or overalls. Faces glazed with cold, collars up as high as they would go, stamping their feet against the gnawing cold, they huddled together. Cigarette smoke occasionally rose from the burning weed held between draws in the cupped hand of the smoker, providing some degree of warmth and comfort.

Spitting, following a racking bout of coughing, always seemed one of the groups' specialities. The men waited in anticipation of some movement from within the yard. Each time the wicket gate opened they glanced up in expectation. Was one of the squads requiring extra hands? Had a key member failed to turn up for that day's work?

But he had been lucky. His Uncle Archie had got him an interview with one of the foremen.

'So, you're Archie MacPhail's nephew. Whit's yer name?' the man had asked.

'Jimmy Muir, sur.'

'Whit does yer faither dae, son?'

'He's deid, sur.'

'Aye, well, yer mother wull be keen fur ye tae bring in a couple o' bob in yer pay-poke, so just you come on Monday morn' an' we'll get ye goin'.'

He could hardly remember what other questions the man had asked, but anyway, here he was. A long line of men were going through a wicket door in the massive gates. He followed them through. The timekeeper stopped him but he explained that he was to start today. He remembered where the foreman who had hired him had told him to go, along a cobbled railway track past the growing ribs of a vessel under construction.

The yard looked neglected with ramshackle huts scattered here and there. His nostrils became aware of oil, smoke, iron and rust, blown aside occasionally with the stiff wind coming from the river. It was grey and cold; dawn had come only an hour before.

A stream of colour suddenly came from welders above, high on a staging against a hull. One stopped and looked down, tipping back his visor and reminding Jimmy of a drawing he had once seen in a history book of Robert the Bruce.

A sudden clang made him jump, then there came a dreadful racket from an engine nearby as it started up. The sky started to move with a sprawl of crane jibs. The place was massive, dirty, and frightening to his senses, unaccustomed to such things. A generator hummed loudly at him as he passed, and he suddenly found himself dodging crackling sparks from a welder's torch. Even the belt fae Curly Wilson might be better than this.

A mountain of massive launching chains lay curled next to an empty slipway, the surface of which was green with seaweed. Looming up was a huge shed, taller than anything he had seen before. A pulley crane worked its way slowly up and down its length, sheets of metal dangling from its hook. As he entered the building the sound and vibration seemed to build to a crescendo. The wintry sky crept past grimy, shattered windows. The ceiling was supported by pillars made from upright steel joists from which the dirty brown paint had bubbled and flaked.

He saw the foreman, Mister Murray, just as the man saw him. 'Right you, Jimmy, come an' meet Neilie. He started last week so he's an expert on building ships,' he said with a huge grin.

Neilie proved to be a lad from Jimmy's old school. Jimmy remembered him. It was so good to see a familiar face in these unfamiliar surroundings.

'Come oan an' ah'll take ye fur a walk under a boat, Jimmy.'

'In a diver's suit?'

'Don't be daft! The thing isnae in the water yet. Sure it's still on the slip'.

'Huv we naw got tae dae some work?' asked Jimmy.

'Naw, we're jist apprentices. Go fur the mens' papers and fags and rolls and such like. We'll get tae work later. Come oan and see this big boat.'

The bottom of the ship in question seemed like a massive steel ceiling, stretching away into the distance, with an occasional deafening noise threatening to topple the whole structure off its supports.

'If this thing falls we're deid,' observed Jimmy.

'It'll no' fall, ya feartie,' replied Neilie. 'They've been building ships like this wan fur years an' years. Anyway, ah'm fair lookin' forward to the launch. They say the Queen might even launch it. Did ye know that the apprentices also get, sort of, launched in this yard?'

'Ye mean thrown in the watter?'

'Ah don't know tae tell you the truth. But ah hear we have got tae go through some sort of wee initiation ceremony.'

Then he remembered well the initiation ceremony for new apprentices. It was 'See You, Jimmy's' turn. He had had to wait outside while other apprentices were 'done'. As he was brought into the shed he could see his pal Neilie standing with his arms folded, a massive grin on his face. 'Ah, well,' thought Jimmy, 'it cannae be that bad.'

Jimmy was made to stand on an old stool and be blindfolded. He was then asked to put both arms on two journeymen's shoulders, either side of him and be hoisted on top of the stool into the air. Suddenly there was a shout from the journeymen. 'Son, we cannae haud ye. Fur heaven's sake jump for it!' Jimmy immediately panicked, his heart raced, and he made a massive breenge of a jump, letting out a scream as he did so. His feet immediately hit the ground. Pulling off the blindfold he looked at the smiling faces. He understood it now. What had happened was that the men had slowly lowered themselves, giving Jimmy the impression that he was ten feet up in the air, when in fact he was only a couple of inches off the ground!

He joined Neilie who gave him a slap on the back. 'Welcome tae the apprentices' club, Jimmy,' he laughed.

Jimmy stood, his heart still thumping. The silly initiation ceremony reminded him of 'dares' carried out during his childhood.

He remembered how his friend Winnie and himself were told by Iain Duncan and his brother Blair, that in order to join their gang they had to go up the stairs in a certain tenement close, and knock on every door as they went up. Then, once they'd knocked on the doors on the top landing, they had to count to 12 before running down the stairs shouting, 'It wisnae me! It wisnae me!'

Jimmy could always remember coming racing down the stairs with Winnie, and being caught by an irate housewife on the bottom landing who stated, 'Aye, it bliddy well wis youse!' and gave them both a brisk clip on the ear.

Anyway, that was his initiation ceremony over, thank goodness. Hopefully he might actually do some work. It would be just great to know that you had made even a wee bit of one of these big ships.

The section Jimmy found himself in with his pal, Neilie, was the blacksmith's shop. A furnace roared at one end and men fought with angled steel to meet the required specifications for various ships' parts. Jimmy and Neilie were sent to work with two blacksmiths and given the task of producing six long ladders for a ship's engine room.

The first ladder, all 30 feet of it, took Jimmy and Neilie a couple of weeks. They red-leaded and painted it black. Apart from one or two rough bits it looked fine. They felt proud. It was stored at the rear of the huge shed.

The other five were made and completed together. Now the boys felt like real shipyard workers. In fact, after making the ladders, as they had done so well, they were assigned to a journeyman working in the area of the ship where the engine would be installed.

One day the blacksmith foreman came to see them on the ship. 'Where's the sixth ladder, Jimmy? We can only find five.'

'We put them aw against the back o' the shed, Mister Murray.'

'Well you had better come and show me.'

The ladder wasn't there. Look and enquire as they might the lads failed to find the ladder. Jimmy was worried. Maybe he would be fired for losing a ladder. His mother would kill him.

Mister Murray the foreman told them gruffly, 'Well, ye will jist need tae make another one. And we need it in a couple o' days. Don't lose this one.'

The ladder was produced in double-quick time, helped by some of the blacksmiths. It was then carried over to the ship.

It was a few days later at the lunch break, that Jimmy overheard two of the blacksmiths talking.

'Naw, it cannae be done.'

'Well, ye can dae it wi' wan, Benny, but no' two.'

'What are you two talking about?' 'See You, Jimmy' asked the men.

'The pennies and the funnel trick, of course,' came the reply.

'Whit's that?' asked 'See you, Jimmy'.

'Well, most folks wi' a bit o' practice can put a penny on wan o' their eyes, and then nod their heid tae get the penny intae a funnel stuck oan their belt,' exclaimed Benny, one of the platers. 'But it would require fantastic eye co-ordination to manage two pennies aff baith eyes intae a funnel.'

'Ah, bet ye ah could do it,' exclaimed the enthusiastic 'See you, Jimmy'. 'Ah wis aye great at heidin' a tennis ball against the dunny wall.'

'Ok, we'll let you hae a go. But ah doubt if you'll manage it.'

Two pennies were put on 'See you, Jimmy''s closed eyelids and a funnel for filling drums stuck in his trousers. Suddenly, 'See You, Jimmy' felt a rush of freezing water pouring down the funnel and into his trousers. He stood, shocked, utterly soaked, and dripping.

'Ya big bastards!' he exclaimed to the grinning duo.

+ + +

At the end of each week in the yard, the men in the plating shed all gave 'See You, Jimmy' two shillings. He was told to go to 'Sweeney Todd's, the local 'whip-it-quick' barber, and get them 'something fur the weekend'.

Puzzled, the apprentice entered the barber's shop, fearing that it was another wee joke being played on him, yet somewhat reassured by the fact he had been given all this money. Jimmy told the barber the men in the shed had asked him to 'get something for the weekend'. He was ushered into the back shop where the shelves were lined with boxes of Durex condoms. The order was duly wrapped up in brown paper. When he came back to the yard he was immediately surrounded by the men wanting their 'French Letters'. Whether the condoms were all used each weekend or whether they were bought as acts of masculine bravado, he never got to know. However, in due time, 'See You, Jimmy' was one of the people placing an order!

His time in the yards had simply flown. He remembered all the ships he had been involved in building. The nonsense they all got up to. The characters he met. Great memories. Then there was his courtship of Helen, the wee girl in the tracing office that had caught his eye. A few of the lads had fancied her, but he could see she was taken with him too. Then there were the strikes, being laid off, and finally redundancy. Thankfully he had found another job almost immediately.

Their three children were now grown up and a grandchild was on the way. Life had had its ups and downs but in the main he had been blessed.

Now it was Jimmy and his Helen's Silver wedding. It seemed that one minute he was just a wee apprentice, and now here he was, on his favourite ship. Of course they had agreed there was only one way they could celebrate. It had cost a few bob but he had always wanted to cross the Atlantic on the *QE2*. After all, sure he had built it. It would be dead romantic and he would be fulfilling a dream.

They flew to New York and embarked from Manhattan; they would be mid-Atlantic on their big day.

The dream began as tugs nudged the QE2 away from the West Manhattan quayside, and the world's most famous skyline unfolded before them. When they peered down at the Hudson River from what felt like the height of a skyscraper, Jimmy once

again sensed the true scale of the ship. Her presence had dominated the yard. The liner eased past the Statue of Liberty, slipped under the graceful Verrazano Narrows Bridge, and headed into open waters, with five days and 3,000 nautical miles ahead.

Jimmy was surprised that he found it difficult at first to find his way around the ship. Then he remembered – when Browns had built the ship it was segregated into three passenger classes. This practice had been since been abandoned and most of the barriers removed.

They found the weather on deck distinctly bracing. Cunard did its best to sustain a facsimile of traditional deck-board life, staging quoits, tennis, shuffleboard and putting contests. Judging the slope on an ever-shifting deck was a challenge. The

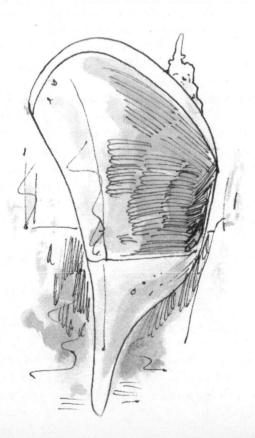

couple also participated in the baggo contest, which entailed throwing beanbags into a 6-inch target hole.

There was never the slightest threat of boredom, with Cunard laying on a stream of indoor pursuits; talks on thriller-writing, cooking, bridge, chess, quizzes, shopping … along with the world's largest floating library. There were exercise classes, dancing and stage shows. Jimmy and Helen even attended a concert where the pianist's rendition of Rachmaninov was superb.

Their anniversary passed with the champagne on Cunard. In the Britannia Grill their gastronomic fantasies were fulfilled. They choose from caviar, smoked salmon, crab, Dover sole, Maine lobster and prime Kansas beef, with ever-watchful waiters enticing them to eat more. It was a magical dinner with sea spume gleaming through the windows.

As they finished their meal, Jimmy thought he saw a face he recognised coming towards them. Older and greyer perhaps, but, right enough, it was Neilie from the yard!

'Neilie, man, whit are you doing here? And you're in uniform.'

'Jimmy, Helen, ah saw yer names on the passenger list. It's grand tae see you. I'm working on the auld ship noo. In fact, you'll laugh, it's ma job tae polish the engines.'

'Neilie, you must come on down to the cabin for a wee dram an' we'll talk about auld times,' suggested Jimmy.

'Jimmy, that'll be grand but ah'm oan duty right noo. Later, eh? But why don't you come doon an' see ma engines. You know they're different fae the wans pit in on the Clyde. Noo we've goat diesel electric. Run like clockwork.'

'Listen, Jimmy,' said Helen, 'you go and see Neilie's engines. Ah'll catch up wi' ye both later.'

'Ok, pet,' replied Jimmy. 'Come oan Neilie lad, you show me your engines an' we'll chat aboot old times.'

The engines proved impressive. Quieter than Jimmy expected they simply throbbed with power. A walkway bridge with ladders running everywhere filled the upper area of the engine room. Officers in white overalls sat monitoring dials and screens. Here was the heart of the vessel. Jimmy felt quite emotional.

'Must keep you fit going up and doon aw they ladders, Neilie,' said Jimmy, his voice slightly raised above the hum of the engines.

'Aye, ah suppose so.'

'Dae ye remember that you and I lost an engine room ladder way back, when we started in the blacksmith's shop?' asked Jimmy.

'Ah certainly do. Did ye ever learn whit happened to it? No. Well all ah can tell you, Jimmy, is that ah wis recently reading a book aboot Glasgow, an' do you know, a prisoner broke oot o' Barlinnie using a thirty foot ladder aboot a week after we loast oors.'

'Heavens above. Who wis he?'

'Remember Mister Murray? Well it wis his brother.'

'Well, ah never! Noo ah know why he didnae seem over-concerned.'

+ + +

The following day, as Helen and Jimmy stood on deck, there was a miraculous seascape, with the sun breaking through storm clouds, the *QE2*'s bows ploughing into the swells as her iridescent wake zigzagged to the horizon. As Jimmy observed, 'Whit a ship! Aw the way fae Clydebank. By heavens, us Scots are a clever lot!'

Oi, Jimmy!